PENGUIN CLASSICS

SUNJATA

BAMBA SUSO (d.1974) was one of the foremost Gambian griots and had an extensive knowledge of local oral traditions.

BANNA KANUTE (d. *circa* 1994) was a renowned musician and griot who played with the Gambia National Troupe.

GORDON INNES researched and wrote about Mande languages and oral literatures during a distinguished career at the School of Oriental and African Studies, University of London.

BAKARI SIDIBE is a Gambian scholar who has worked extensively on Mandinka oral literature.

LUCY DURÁN writes on African music, particularly from the Mande cultural world, and teaches at the School of Oriental and African Studies.

GRAHAM FURNISS writes on African oral and written literatures and is a specialist on Hausa. He also teaches at the School of Oriental and African Studies.

SUNJATA

*Gambian Versions of the Mande Epic
by Bamba Suso and Banna Kanute*

Translated and annotated by GORDON INNES
with the assistance of BAKARI SIDIBE

*Edited, with a new introduction and additional notes
by* LUCY DURÁN *and* GRAHAM FURNISS

PENGUIN BOOKS

PENGUIN BOOKS

Published by the Penguin Group
Penguin Books Ltd, 27 Wrights Lane, London w8 5tz, England
Penguin Putnam Inc., 375 Hudson Street, New York, New York 10014, USA
Penguin Books Australia Ltd, Ringwood, Victoria, Australia
Penguin Books Canada Ltd, 10 Alcorn Avenue, Toronto, Ontario, Canada m4v 3b2
Penguin Books (NZ) Ltd, Private Bag 102902, NSMC, Auckland, New Zealand

Penguin Books Ltd, Registered Offices: Harmondsworth, Middlesex, England

These translations first published in *Sunjata: Three Mandinka Versions* by the
School of Oriental and African Studies 1974
Published with a new introduction and additional material in Penguin Classics 1999
10 9 8 7 6 5 4 3 2 1

Text and notes copyright © Gordon Innes, 1974 and 1999
Introduction and additional material copyright © Lucy Durán and Graham Furniss, 1999

Set in 10/12.5 pt Monotype Bembo
Typeset by Rowland Phototypesetting Ltd, Bury St Edmunds, Suffolk
Printed in England by Clays Ltd, St Ives plc

Contents

Introduction

During the years between the Norman conquest of England and the reign of Henry VIII (*c.* 1066–1547), the world saw many empires rise and fall. Europe's high Middle Ages saw the rise and decline of the Holy Roman Empire, the establishment of the Spanish Christian kingdoms of Castile, Leon, Aragon and Navarre, the Crusades, and the rise across Europe of a nascent bourgeoisie alongside the feudal nobility and the peasants. Elsewhere in the world, contemporaneously with the Sung dynasty in China and the Kamakura period in Japan, Muslim control was extended to North India as well as into Spain and North Africa, under the Abbasids and their successors.

In West Africa meanwhile, three great empires rose and fell, the empires of Ghana, Mali and Songhai. Ghana was famed in the 11th century throughout the Arab world as a producer of gold, gold which was traded across the desert from the heartland of the empire in the upper reaches of the Senegal river to North Africa and beyond. At its height (*c.* 1050) the empire stretched from the Niger bend to what is now middle Senegal, and from the desert across the savanna. The empire of Mali arose after the disintegration of the Ghana empire into a series of smaller competing states. Under the great Mansa (king) Musa, who made a famous visit to Mecca in 1324, the empire of Mali stretched from Senegal to Timbuktu and Gao in the present-day Republic of Mali. The third great empire, that of Songhai, reached its zenith under Askia Muhammad in the 1520s.

The epic narrative in this book is about the beginnings of the empire of Mali in the early thirteenth century. It concerns the struggle by Mande-speaking people for independence from rule by a Susu king. An Arab historian of the period said,

The authority of the rulers of Ghana dwindled away, and they fell under the domination of the Sosso people – their Sudanese neighbours – who subdued and crushed them completely. Later, the people of Mali, increasing in population more than any of the Sudanese nations, overran the whole region. They vanquished the Sosso, and took all their possessions, both their ancient kingdom and that of Ghana, as far as the ocean to the West.[1]

The Susu/Sosso people had been subjects of the Ghana empire until, in alliance with other groups, they were able to assert their independence. During the twelfth century Susu extended its authority to incorporate territories of old Ghana and Mande chieftaincies. Early in the 13th century the greatest king of the Susu, Sumanguru Kante, found himself confronted by a revolt of the Mande-speaking peoples under his control led by Sunjata. The victory of Sunjata over Sumanguru put an end to the Susu kingdom and began the establishment of the great Mali empire over a large part of the West African savanna.

The Sunjata epic in all its varied and various forms relates aspects of this history. N. Levtzion summarizes the Arabic chronicler, Ibn Khaldun, and oral tradition as follows:

Sundjata, an exiled prince from a Malinke [Mande] chiefdom on the Sankarani (a tributary of the Upper Niger, on the border between modern Guinea and Mali), was called back by his people to free the country from the yoke of Sumanguru Kante, the oppressive king of Sosso. A collation of various traditions suggests that Sundjata had first endeavoured to unite under his authority the different Malinke chiefdoms, both by contracting treaties of alliance and by coercion. At the head of the united force of the Malinke, Sundjata defeated the powerful Sumanguru. The combat between the two great warriors is presented by the oral traditions as a struggle between two powerful magicians.[2]

The 'oral tradition' is, of course, never a single source and never the same story. The closest to an integrated narrative is perhaps that created by the Guinean scholar D. T. Niane in 1965. Niane was writing for an international audience, creating a prose synthesis from a number of performances by the same jali (griot). We summarize below the narrative as he renders it in his book, *Sundiata: an Epic of Old Mali*,[3] but with names as they occur in the Mandinka versions given in this volume.

The story

In the early thirteenth century, the Mande people were organized into many small kingdoms, such as Sibi, Kita, Neema, among others. Sunjata's father, Naareng Makhang Konnate, was king in Niani, within Manding, in what is now eastern Guinea. He already had two wives, but was advised to take a third wife, Sukulung Konte, who was an ugly hunchback and a buffalo-woman, because it was predicted she would give birth to a great ruler who would bring the Mande to great power. She was a princess of the kingdom of Do. Sukulung Konte proved a good wife but was the object of much hatred and jealousy from her co-wives. Sunjata was born to her just before the birth of a half-brother to a co-wife; Sunjata's mother sent a slave to announce his birth at the court, while a griot was sent to announce the half-brother's arrival. The griot made his announcement before the slave did, so Sunjata was considered the younger brother and not eligible for the throne.

Sunjata Keita ('the lion-thief who takes his inheritance'), Sukulung Konte's eldest son, started life as a cripple and a glutton who at the age of seven was still crawling. After several years of being tormented by his step-mothers, Sunjata finally pulled himself up on to his own two feet by uprooting a baobab tree. Thereafter, Sunjata became renowned and feared for his superhuman strength, brilliant archery and remarkable bravery.

When his father died, life in Manding became difficult for Sunjata. All he asked for as his inheritance was his father's jali, Bala Faasigi Kuyate. But Sunjata's half-brother had been proclaimed king and had taken Bala Faasigi Kuyate to be his own personal musician. In desperation, Sunjata went into exile with his mother, taking refuge in the kingdom of Neema. Here Sunjata trained for battle, and gradually the word spread far and wide telling of the extraordinary abilities of this young warrior and hunter.

Meanwhile Sumanguru Kante, king of the Susu people and a famed blacksmith and powerful sorcerer, annexed the kingdom of Manding causing Sunjata's half-brother to flee. Sumanguru captured Bala Faasigi Kuyate, Sunjata's musician. Sumanguru kept a xylophone (*bala*) in his inner chamber, but one day Bala Faasigi – who had previously only played the drums – made his way into the chamber and picked up the *bala*. The music he played on it was so sweet that Sumanguru Kante nicknamed him Bala Faasigi, 'praise on the xylophone', and from then on the xylophone became one of the principal instruments of the Mande jali.

When Sunjata heard the news of Sumanguru's annexation of Manding, he prepared to return home from exile in Neema, following the death of his mother. Back in Manding he was joined by the army of Faa Koli Dumbuya, Sumanguru's nephew, who had defected to Sunjata's side because Sumanguru had stolen his wife from him. Sumanguru's strength lay in his occult power, but Sunjata's sister seduced him and forced him to betray the secret of his vulnerability. The remainder of the story concerns the many fierce battles that ensued between Sumanguru and Sunjata using the arts of sorcery. Gradually all the kings of Manding pledged allegiance to Sunjata and fought at his side. One of Sunjata's generals, Tira Makhang, was sent to conquer the kingdoms of Wolof in the west, and founded the Mandinka kingdom in Kaabu (now Guinea Bissau). At the battle of Kirina, Sunjata finally overwhelmed Sumanguru with a magic arrow; Sumanguru was chased into the east and vanished. Manding was at last restored to its rightful ruler under whom all the smaller kingdoms united, becoming one of Africa's most powerful empires for the next two centuries.

The telling of the story

. . . The Sunjata story
Is very strange and wonderful.
You see one griot,
And he gives you an account of it one way,
And you will find that that is the way he heard it;
You see another griot,
And he gives you an account of it in another way,
And you will find that what he has heard has determined his version.
What I have myself heard,

What I have heard from my parents,
That is the account which I will put before you. (6–16)

The story of Sunjata Keita has come to be one of the world's greatest living epic oral traditions. These opening lines by the Mandinka musician Banna Kanute, in his recitation of Sunjata for Gordon Innes in 1970, are an almost textbook view of the nature of 'epic' performance. That it is 'strange and wonderful' is evident from the fact that after more than seven and a half centuries, it continues to be a living concern for the millions of West African peoples generally referred to as Mande. Mande (sometimes called Manding) is a term covering a number of closely related languages, spoken by peoples who trace their ancestry to Sunjata's empire. The heartland language of present-day Guinea and western Mali is Maninka (French: *Malinké*), and the westernmost variant is Mandinka, spoken in the Gambia, southern Senegal and Guinea Bissau. Another of the major Mande languages is Bamana (French: *Bambara*).

The figure of Sunjata (French: *Soundiata*) is an important cultural symbol for Mande peoples (comparable in some ways to Richard the Lionheart for the English). But the Sunjata story is not some quaint relic of a bygone era: it forms part of an extensive and vibrant oral tradition of Mande epic stories and praise songs that are constantly being regenerated through new performance. This tradition has been kept alive by highly skilled professional musicians who are known by the Mandinka term 'jali' (Maninka and Bamana: *jeli*, *djeli*), often translated as griot, bard or 'master of the word'. The texts in this volume were recited by Bamba Suso and Banna Kanute, two master jalis in the Mandinka cultural tradition of the Gambia.

Not only have jalis been the guardians of Sunjata's history, they also figure prominently in the story itself, as we can see from the two versions presented here. Their oral traditions provide the main, but not the only source of information on the early Mande courts. By the fourteenth century, there are also written accounts, which confirm that jalis played a crucial role: the Moroccan, Ibn Battuta, who visited Mansa Sulayman's court in 1352 describes the jali as interpreter, public orator, poet, and genealogist, and provider of music for festivities. He refers to Dugha, the king's jali, as 'one of the respected and important Sudan' (i.e. people of the western savannah). His description of the pomp and grandeur of the king's musical ensemble, with Dugha playing a xylophone, backed by a hundred-strong female chorus in fine clothes and decked in gold and silver,[4] could well apply to the 1990s in the areas where Mande traditions have remained strongest, particularly western Mali, except that, if it were Mali today, there would also be microphones, amplifiers, electric guitars, and even drum machines, to add to the spectacle.

The texts presented in this volume

Bamba Suso and Banna Kanute addressed these texts to audiences who were familiar with the story. They assumed knowledge, knowledge not only of the story lines, and of the characters who moved in and out of the narrative, but also of the many different versions of what the central characters were like, their personalities and their histories. People are introduced into the story on the assumption that the audience already knows them. Dialogue takes place which, in performance, evokes all the overtones of emotion and meaning that are the product of past performances. In introducing these two texts to our present audience we set out some of the characteristics which we see as significant in these two versions, not in order to represent the 'story' definitively, but to flesh out what we see as being conveyed in sometimes the briefest of elements in the texts.

Sunjata is, in these two versions, a man destined for greatness. Prior to his birth he is marked out as different. But the circumstances of his birth and his youth are hardly glorious. Bamba Suso presents a picture of Sunjata as a crippled child, unable to compete with his peers or accomplish simple tasks for his mother as any other growing boy would be expected to do. As he grows, his frustration and anger at his position lead him to be quick to take offence and to seek vengeance. His mother is publicly ridiculed for her disabled child. Her isolation and humiliation, in Banna Kanute's version, is reinforced by the fact that Sunjata's older brothers have all been killed, fighting for the Prophet Muhammad. For

Bamba Suso, there is a close and deep relationship between Sunjata and his mother. Faced with a choice, later in the story, between becoming king or staying to care for his aged and infirm mother, Sunjata chooses the latter. Faced with the mocking of his mother by other women, in Banna Kanute's version, Sunjata comforts her and tells her not to be so upset, he will by himself accomplish the task that will show them how capable he really is. When rods of iron have buckled under his weight as Sunjata endeavours to pull himself upright, it is his mother who is the rock upon which he finally pulls himself to a standing position. It is not only fate which has been cruel to Sunjata as a child; in Bamba Suso's version, the announcement of the birth of Sunjata, which would have led to his nomination as his father's heir, is delivered to the court minutes after the announcement of the slightly later birth of the child of a co-wife, who is thus considered the heir. It is a griot, a central figure in Sunjata's life, who is the agent of this usurpation, and Sunjata's frustration and anger at this unfairness is given, by Bamba Suso, as one of the causes of his insistence on continuing to crawl when other children have learned to walk. Not only is he crippled, he is marked out by having spent years in his mother's womb before birth. His closeness to his mother is at one moment endangered; her position as dutiful and virtuous wife is threatened when Sunjata comes to understand that she once 'had a fright', that she had once committed a dishonourable act, only to discover that the incident was entirely innocuous. Nevertheless, his quick anger at the potential humiliation leads him to threaten to kill his mother and himself – a most serious threat, indicating what a man of extremes he is.

In Banna Kanute's version, Sunjata's mother is well beyond child-bearing age when she gives birth to Sunjata; she is miraculously restored to youth by the intervention of the Prophet for whose cause forty of the sons of Sunjata's father have given their lives. Presented with a picture of a companionable old age shared by Sunjata's mother and father, we see the demise of Sunjata's father leading his mother into a life of hardship; alone with her daughter and her crippled son, she turns for help to the ruling king, Sumanguru, whose smiths fashion the iron rods intended to allow Sunjata to arise. Sunjata laughs at these attempts to help him, knowing that when destiny decrees that he will rise he will do so using his own extraordinary strength. It is one of the ironies of Banna Kanute's version that Sumanguru arranges to help the person who is destined to defeat him in the end.

The significance of Sunjata's mother is matched, if not exceeded, by the role played in the progress of the story by his sister, Nene Faamaga. The crucial roles of these two women, combined with the counter-vailing presence at a later point of Sumanguru's mother, are a major feature of the whole story. Where Sunjata's mother was ill-looking, his sister was, according to Bamba Suso, 'the best-looking woman in both Susu and Manding' (697), a woman of calming influence, of initiative, courage and sharp wit. Not only does she, Nene Faamaga, instil patience and self-control in Sunjata when he is angry, it is her seductive power and her cool head which leads, at her initiative, to Sunjata's victory.

The strength of Sunjata's devotion and loyalty to his mother is measured by the cold fury of his reaction to an erstwhile ally's demand that Sunjata pay for his mother's burial plot after her death. Caught in the obligations of guest to host he has to pay but, in language replete with symbolism, he vows one day to have his revenge.

Sunjata's loyalty to his sister encompasses the skated-over implication that an incestuous relationship has taken place between her and another brother who forced her into a sexual liaison. Sunjata's reaction is to disqualify the brother from any chance of succeeding to the throne. Nene Faamaga's loyalty to Sunjata remains absolute, both in Bamba Suso's version where she is unmarried, and in Banna Kanute's where she is married to a spirit king.

In Bamba Suso's version, it is in exile that Sunjata makes the transition from hot-head to mature hero. Sunjata waits patiently to assemble his armies, carefully laying his plans before attacking Sumanguru. Rivalry, potential or actual, between Sunjata's military commanders is obviated by his ability to unite and maintain a powerful coalition among his generals, including the important figure of Faa Koli who defects from Sumanguru's camp when Sumanguru seduces his wife. For Bamba Suso there is a balance between the 'man of words' (ngara) and the 'man of action' (ngana; the jali-defined origin of the name Ghana), summed up in the personality of Sunjata. Sunjata was both, but spoke often through his griot, Bala Faasigi, another key figure in most versions of Sunjata.

There is a depth of devotion and commitment between Sunjata and Bala Faasigi in Bamba Suso's version which is not so apparent in Banna Kanute's. Sunjata declares that of all his inheritance it is the griots he wishes to retain. He goes to extraordinary lengths to maintain his griot and to see to his daily needs, a relationship built upon the dependence of the griot upon his patron. The griot for his part both tells Sunjata's story and sings his praises, protecting the interests of his patron. As with all such patron–client relationships, the client can remain potentially fickle, able to change allegiance according to circumstance. Where Bamba Suso's version portrays mutual devotion, Banna Kanute's has Bala Faasigi first attached to Sumanguru, and only much later does he become Sunjata's griot, forced, according to Banna Kanute, to remain with him and to play for him upon the xylophone.

As with many epic narratives, the series of conflicts representing the historical military clashes between armies is played out through the encounter of individuals. In this case Sunjata against Sumanguru. In this regard, however, the two versions presented here differ markedly. In Bamba Suso's version, battle is joined between Sunjata's maternal grandfather and Sumanguru's jinn father, in circumstances where the secret invulnerability of Sumanguru and his father has been discovered. Sumanguru's final disappearance in this version is set within a sequence of supernatural changes, emphasizing the magical powers that have underpinned Sumanguru's dominance and finally also Sunjata's victory. In Banna Kanute's version, the story reaches a climax in hand-to-hand combat between the two main protagonists in which the secret invulnerability finally produces Sumanguru's undoing.

This latter feature, the presence of supernatural beings, powers and actions, constitutes the prime focus of Banna Kanute's version. The excitement of Banna Kanute's narrative lies in the violent action and the magic with which the story is imbued. Diviners are set by Sumanguru to discover the presence of the child who will be a threat to his sovereignty, and each act of divination produces a symbolic conflict (between chickens, rams and other metaphorical representations) in which the element representing Sumanguru is always defeated. Sumanguru will not accept the inevitability of this destiny and seeks to thwart it. He employs magical powers in his attempt both to protect himself against and to defeat Sunjata. But it is when he is at his most vulnerable, naked in the washing area, that he is surprised by Sunjata and forced to destroy his protective amulets and his offensive magical substances. Sunjata himself has been assisted by the spirit-king husband of his sister, who transports Sunjata and his sister through the air to take Sumanguru by surprise.

Perhaps the most graphic and striking episode in both these versions is the scene in which Sunjata's sister, Nene Faamaga, seduces Sumanguru into revealing his secret invulnerability. The subtlety of Bamba Suso's version stands in contrast with the directness of that of Banna Kanute. The contrast between the two versions highlights the way in which oral traditions contain within them not only the potential for infinite variety in rendering character and plot, but also the potential to accommodate the differing interests of the reciters, reflecting their own personalities and predilections. In Bamba Suso we see the hinting at subtleties in human interaction expressed through dialogue, and in Banna Kanute we see a fascination with the supernatural, the excitement of action, and the accumulation of power in all its forms, natural and supernatural.

The jalis

The 'jali' as a social institution dates back at least to the time of Sunjata, and has been, and remains, a cornerstone of Mande culture. Mande society consists of three broad social categories: the *horon* (Mandinka: *foro*), who are the 'freeborn' – roughly equivalent to nobility – descended from rulers, and not attached to any particular occupation; the *nyamakala* (Mandinka: *nyamalo*), those who are born into certain professions or trades, for example music and other specialized verbal and performance arts (the jali); and the *jon* (Mandinka: *jong*), descendants of slaves and captives. There is, still today, little intermarriage between these groups, which represent a form of social hierarchy, with the *nyamakala* in the middle. In pre-colonial days, it was the freeborn who were the patrons of jalis. A particular family of jalis would remain for generations with a freeborn family, and thus they acquired detailed knowledge of the genealogies and family histories of their patrons. One of the main functions of jalis is to sing or recite family histories and lineages on ritual occasions, and the story of Sunjata is an example of this type of recitation. Part of this verbal art consists of reciting the 'praise names' of a family – with extensive use of obscure epithets such as 'cats on the shoulder', not always directly understood, but often representing some episode from an important moment in the family history. These names have the effect of heightening the emotional tension of a narrative (without necessarily advancing the story), and Mande listeners who are praised in this way by a skilled jali will often reward them generously.

The jali has many other important ritual and social functions. He or she acts as go-between during disputes, as confidential adviser on many matters ranging from business to marriage, and as public spokesperson. For example, it is still uncommon in the Gambia today for a local chief or other dignitary to raise his or her voice at a public meeting. Instead, the message will be passed in low tones to a jali, who will then proclaim the announcement, often embellishing the original words.

Parts of the Mande world, especially near the heartland, have been Islamic since the time of Sunjata. The Mandinka, however, were among the last group of Mande to be converted to Islam, a process which did not fully take place until the end of the 19th century. Their practice of Islam therefore retains many aspects of pre-Islamic belief in esoteric power, and this is amply reflected in the two Sunjata texts in this book. Thus, we find in these narratives that the religious clerics, locally known as marabouts, are continually called upon by both Sunjata and Susu Sumanguru to fabricate power-objects such as amulets, as well as to engage in various forms of divination. Banna Kanute, in particular, relies heavily on stories of esoteric power as a central part of his narration.

Although colonialism has undermined traditional systems of kingship, jalis continue to fulfil an important social role in contemporary Mande society, throughout the Mande diaspora. Virtually any ceremonial or festive occasion requires the presence of a jali: their music is the ubiquitous backdrop to weddings, child-naming parties, religious festivities, national holidays, even political rallies. Their praise songs in memory of former kings and warriors – often adapted to honour leading members of contemporary society such as businessmen and politicans

– fill the airwaves of radio and television stations. The most famous of these jalis, especially in Mali and Guinea, sometimes receive gifts from their patrons of extraordinary generosity: money, houses, cars, land, even, in the case of one female singer, a small airplane.[5] They dress in beautiful long robes of damask, tie-dye, or embroidered cloth. They are symbols of traditional Mande values in the modern world.

Most recently, since the early 1980s, jalis have extended their audiences to include the international concert circuit, and have moved into new areas of musical performance such as popular music. Dance bands from Guinea and Mali have recorded versions of Sunjata, with arrangements of the very same tunes that Banna Kanute and Bamba Suso used to accompany their recitations. Another Sunjata tune, one that is sung to proclaim his bravery ('Death is better than disgrace'), was adopted as the Mali national anthem. The Gambia National Troupe, the government-sponsored state ensemble (of which Banna Kanute was once a member) often begins its performances with Sunjata.

Thus the Sunjata story circulates widely in various guises. Full-length epic recitations, however, are now rare. They tend to be reserved for special, ceremonial occasions such as the re-roofing of the sacred hut (*kamablon*) in Kangaba (Mali), and only certain jalis are authorized to participate in the performance. To our knowledge, no such ritual or commemorative occasions exist in the Gambia, being far away from the Mande heartland. Instead, the most likely contexts in which a long version of Sunjata might be recited are the *sumungolu*. These are private informal gatherings held in the evening at a patron's house, in which the jali sits and recites stories, with musical accompaniment, for the patron's edification and entertainment. The atmosphere at such gatherings can be highly charged, with frequent interruptions and excited exclamations of 'It's true!', as the jali evokes the great heroes of the past through song.

The fact that both texts in this volume were specially requested by Gordon Innes can be seen as an extension of the traditional performance context. Jalis are, above all, professionals who are used to adapting to different types of audience and patron, including researchers. Innes was, in effect, taking the role of patron. The use of the word 'text' here needs some further explanation. These line-by-line translations of two single performances do not represent a 'definitive' Sunjata, and were never intended to do so, as Banna Kanute himself implies in the lines quoted above. The story of Sunjata is a fluid concept, constructed around a series of episodes and characters. The art of the jali lies in his or her ability to re-create and adapt elements from the Sunjata story (and other story-songs from the Mande repertoire) to suit the occasion. It might be only a fragment of the story that is sung – interspersed with praise names of the Keita lineage; or it may be a single episode narrated. This is particularly the case with published recordings, because of the constraints of time. For example, in talking about the version by the Guinean singer Mory Kante, recorded in 1975 with the Malian dance orchestra, the Rail Band, Kante describes the Sunjata story as divided into three 'episodes', the Birth, the Exile and the Return, each of which can be sung as a self-contained story. In the Rail Band recording, he sings only 'The Exile'.

The fact that singers like Mory Kante and Salif Keita have performed versions of Sunjata in non-traditional styles and for performance at nightclubs and concert venues is testimony to the endurance of the jali tradition. It has ensured that the music of the jalis is listened to and appreciated by vast audiences across West Africa and further afield.

The 'performance modes'

As with all great story-telling traditions, the jali exploits a number of vocal techniques or performance styles to capture the audience's attention. Gordon Innes, in the original introduction,[6] called these 'modes', a term which has since gone into wide usage with other scholars. Before discussing these, it is perhaps worth emphasizing that these texts were meant to be heard, not read, with all the force and nuance of the spoken and sung word, as delivered by two master practitioners. Pace is extremely variable: a page of text in this book may represent as little as two minutes of performance time or even less, since the jalis tend to recite faster than the normal pace of everyday speech, especially in recitation mode. As Innes said in his introduction: 'the speed of utterance varies . . . sometimes it is so extremely rapid

that it hardly seems humanly possible for speech to be articulated at
such a rate.'[7] Each line of these Mandinka texts, whether spoken (in
the case of Bamba Suso) or spoken and sung (in the case of Banna
Kanute), was given a dramatic inflexion – they started high up and loud
in the vocal register, gradually descending in pitch and strength until a
breath was taken, and the next phrase began. If the text is read with
this in mind, then the frequent repetitions (a device common to most
oral literature) can be 'heard' as a kind of musical rhyme.

The three 'modes' to which Innes refers are speech, recitation and
song. The text here shows the transition from speech to recitation or
song by the use of roman, semi-bold and italic (see Note on Text for
a fuller explanation). Speech and recitation are also generally distinguished from each other by pace and content: the speech mode is closest
to the pace of ordinary speech, and is used to narrate the story. Recitation
on the other hand functions like a parenthesis in the story. It consists
mainly of praise names, such as the standard praise for Sunjata, 'cats on
the shoulder, Simbong [the master hunter] and Jata [the lion] are
at Naarena'. It may also contain references to persons present, or
metaphorical observations on life and human nature, such as 'the world
does not belong to one person' (inveighing against arrogance and
pointing out that even kings must die), or 'being dragged does not
humiliate a beast' (valour). Such recitations consist largely of formulae
that are common to the entire jali repertoire, and indeed often occur
in other story-songs.

Both speech and recitation are free-flowing, in no fixed rhythm.
Song, on the other hand, the third vocal 'mode', consists of fixed
choruses or refrains in steady metre, with a repeated melody. Most of
these are well known to Mande audiences. Such songs would normally
be performed by a chorus of female jalis. Innes's texts in the present
volume indicate these songs by the use of italics; an example is by Banna
Kanute:

> *Sir, it is of Lion that I speak, great stock,*
> *Simbong, it is of Lion that I speak, the man of great stock is a man of power.*
> (1251–2)

This is one of the most popular and widely sung refrains of the Sunjata repertoire. These songs enhance the narrative at particularly dramatic points in the story, for example when Sunjata finally stands on his own two feet.

Although Innes identified three modes of vocal delivery, it is interesting to note that the Mandinka jalis themselves do not differentiate between pure speech and sung recitation. These are both referred to as *sataro* (narration, story-telling). The fixed choruses are known as *donkilo* (literally, 'call to the dance' – because of the steady rhythm).

The music and the musical instruments

Traditionally, the jalis accompany their songs on instruments in which they specialize: the *balafon* (xylophone), also known as *bala*, or *balo*; the *kontingo* (a small lute with up to five strings), also known as *ngoni*; and the *kora* (a large 21-string harp-lute). Certain percussion instruments are also specific to the jalis: the *tama* (a variable pitch drum, held under the arm and struck with a curved stick), the *dundungo* (a large cylindrical drum, also struck with a curved stick) and the *neo* (an iron percussion rod, the only instrument played by the female jalis). These instruments can be played on their own or in mixed ensembles.

Of the three melody instruments, the oldest is the *balafon*. It was the instrument of Sunjata's own jali, hence his nickname 'Bala'. It is not, however, widely played in the Gambia, being more common in Guinea. It has around eighteen keys made of rosewood, which are smoke-dried, and the ends are chiselled to fix the pitches of the 7-note scale. Each key has a hollowed gourd tuned to the same pitch, suspended underneath for extra resonance. Traditionally, the *bala* players attach bells to their wrists, which add an extra percussive effect as they strike the keys.

In the oral traditions of the jalis, musical instruments are closely associated with the world of spirits and jinns. The xylophone, we hear from Banna Kanute, was first played by a spirit king, Manga Yira, the night before the young Sunjata was to emerge from circumcision (1273). The 21-string *kora* was also, according to Bamba Suso, created by the jinns (13–16).

One of the earliest written references to the Mande xylophone and lute was in 1352 by Ibn Battuta. The *kora* on the other hand is not mentioned until 1797, by the Scots traveller Mungo Park, and it developed specifically within the Mandinka cultural area, possibly some 300 years ago. It is a cross between a harp and a lute, with a large half-calabash resonator covered in cow skin, which acts as the sound table. Its distinguishing feature is a raised notched bridge standing at right angles to the sound table. The twenty-one strings are divided into two parallel rows, played with the thumbs and index fingers of both hands, in alternate motion.

The three melody instruments share the same repertoires, consisting mostly of '4-bar' tunes, which provide the framework for instrumental variation, and for the vocal narrative and song. At times, there are florid, virtuoso improvisations, sometimes extending over several cyclical repetitions of the basic melody, much like jazz or blues. The accompaniment plays a vital role in several ways. First, it acts as a reference point for the narration. The jali paces his or her singing or spoken recitation to fit into a certain point in the tune. Second, each tune in the Mande repertoire is associated with a particular episode or character. As they are played over and over again, most Mande listeners are familiar with these tunes, which have strong historical associations. The story of Sunjata has a dozen or more such tunes, each one of which may also be performed in its own right. Thus, when Banna Kanute says:

> This tune which I am playing
> Is one which was played to Sunjata in Manding.
> This tune was played to Faa Koli Kumba and Faa Koli Daaba.
> He was a fierce warrior of Sunjata's (131–4)

he is signalling an important change of accompaniment: from *Kura* (one of the standard tunes for Sunjata; *kura* means 'new', i.e. the newly rebuilt Mande, after the battle) to *Janjungo*, a tune that is dedicated to Fa Koli Dumbuya, the nephew of Sumanguru Kante, who later defected to Sunjata's army. *Janjungo* is considered a serious, almost dangerous, song in praise of the greatest warriors. The jalis believe that only elder musicians have the right to play this piece. The music is thus used as a parallel device to the words as a means of evoking history and sentiment. There are now hundreds of recordings of *balafon* and *kora*, including some of the Sunjata tunes, and from these the reader can capture a sense of how the music actually sounds.

The place of Innes's work in the research on Sunjata

When Gordon Innes set out in 1970 to record these two musicians (with the help of Bakari Sidibe), research on the Mande jalis and on the Sunjata tradition was in its infancy. The importance of the Sunjata story as one of the world's major oral epic traditions was only just becoming known. Most previous versions had been written down in prose form, and mainly came from the Mande heartland, in present-day eastern Guinea and western Mali. Little was known of how Gambian Mandinka versions of Sunjata might correspond to or differ from these.

Innes's work on Sunjata was important, indeed pioneering, for a number of reasons. First, it acknowledged the importance of a line-by-line transcription of an actual performance. The only contemporary publication of Sunjata in wide circulation at the time was that of the Guinean historian D. T. Niane. Though based on the oral testimony of a Guinean griot, Jeli Mamadu Kouyate, it was substantially rewritten and reconstructed in prose style to suit a western readership. Niane's version is regarded by many as an authoritative source for the study of Sunjata, but it differs fundamentally from Innes's approach. The line-by-line translation, according to D. C. Conrad, gives 'the most accurate possible reproduction of the bard's discourse',[8] with its rhetorical devices such as repetition, diversions into song, lengthy praise names and etiological explanations of Mande cultural traditions. Innes carefully recorded all of these, including the use of words and phrases that neither he nor Bakari Sidibe were able to translate: these were sometimes obscure retentions from the 'eastern' (*tilibonko*, as they call it in Gambia) language which is mostly Maninka (see, for example, Banna Kanute 1071, 1082 and 1753).

In fact, it is precisely some of this linguistic evidence which provides important links with the Malian tradition. Some of the place names mentioned, located in present-day Mali (such as Naarena and Dakhajala), were unknown to Innes. At that time, the current thinking was that Niani was the Mande 'capital', while more recent research by Conrad, based partly on Bamba Suso's text, points to Dakhajala as a centre. By documenting the circumstances of the performance, including who was present, Innes was signalling the importance of knowing the context in order to understand the text itself. Both the jalis he recorded, Bamba Suso and Banna Kanute, were above all master performers who worked with (and on) their audiences. Innes arranged for Suso to perform for a crowd of schoolchildren in Brikama, a large multi-ethnic town in western Gambia. He would necessarily have focused on elements of the story that would most appeal to young listeners, such as the use of sorcery. His text is highly didactic in nature. Banna Kanute, on the other hand, was invited to perform at Innes's own house in Serrekunda to a small group of people. This may seem an untraditional setting, but in fact it approximates the *sumungo*, the evening social gathering at the patron's house.

Innes's explanation of the 'performance modes' was also pioneering; they have since been often quoted by other scholars. Banna Kanute has much greater recourse to recitation and song mode as compared with Bamba Suso. These modes have since been used as a basis for analysis by other scholars.[9] Another reason why Innes's work was so important was that most of the versions of Sunjata, both before and since, have drawn on Maninka traditions from the Mande heartland. The story of Sunjata relates specifically to this area, located on the border between present-day Mali and Guinea, which is still today the acknowledged centre of expertise on Sunjata. Within the wider Mande diaspora, it is these Gambian Mandinka narratives recorded by Innes that are now acknowledged to be the closest to those same 'heartland' traditions, despite the geographical and linguistic separation of the two. These versions therefore show a remarkable tenacity in the jali performance tradition.

Innes acknowledged the emerging role of the media in bringing the Mande jali tradition to a wider audience. In his introduction he mentions how jalis such as Banna Kanute had regular radio programmes. Since the early 1970s there has been a proliferation of recordings of jalis' music from the entire Mande cultural world, representing a wide variety of musical styles, from the most 'classical' or 'traditional' to hi-tech pop and fusions with string quartets and jazz bands. Among these recordings, several versions of Sunjata have been published, either as instrumental melodies or with some form of recitation of the story. In this way, Sunjata has become more widely known, though how such recordings interact with the oral tradition is a more complex issue. In any case, as musicians who have acquired specialized professional skills over many generations, the jalis have made the transition into the modern world of technology and mass communication with consummate ease.

Meanwhile, the influential novel *Roots*, by the African–American author Alex Haley, focused worldwide attention on the Gambia and captured the public imagination, to such an extent that the term 'griot' has become synonymous with story-telling and oral literature, and emblematic of African culture. Haley's portrayal of the griot's key role in his dramatic quest for African–American roots back to the African continent was also seen in a major television series that was broadcast around the world.

A feature film 'Keita! Voice of the Griot', directed by Dani Kouyate, tells the story of a jali (the part is actually played by a jali, Sotigui Kouyate) who visits a family called Keita living abroad. The parents are dismissive of the jali, but the young son gradually becomes enthralled by the griot's vivid tale of the exploits of his famous warrior-king ancestor.

However, access to recording and the media is not only a feature of the 1980s and 90s. Both Bamba Suso and Banna Kanute had themselves been exposed to a wide variety of recordings of different jalis, not just from the Gambia but also from Guinea and Mali. Banna Kanute made a number of 78 rpm records when in London in the 1950s, with a small ensemble of Mandinka jalis. They are intriguingly labelled 'Banna Kanute and his Gambia Highlife Cats', although the term 'highlife' (a popular dance style of the 1950s and 60s) is misleading, as the style is quite different from Ghanaian highlife.

Bamba Suso and Banna Kanute

At the time that Innes was doing his research, Bamba Suso and Banna Kanute were considered to be among the leading exponents of the *tilibo* (eastern Mandinka) tradition. Both came from pedigree jali families in eastern Gambia, and had been trained in *tilibo* style. *Tilibo*, literally 'sunrise', is the Mandinka way of referring to the general area east of the Gambia, hence the frequent term 'easterners' in these texts. During the nineteenth and early twentieth centuries, many jalis left the Maninka heartland in western Mali to settle in the upper-river kingdoms of the Gambia. Naturally, they brought with them a Maninka style of music, and Maninka language/dialect in their song texts. Gradually, Maninka and other 'eastern' dialects have fallen out of everyday conversational use, but many phrases and words are retained in the song texts, as is the Maninka melodic style. All of this is broadly referred to, in Gambian Mandinka, as *tilibonko* music.

In the Gambia today, nearly thirty years after Innes made his recordings, the 'classical' and historical repertoire of *tilibo* is giving way to more recent, local forms of Mandinka music, known as *tiliji*, 'sunset' (i.e. from the western part of the country). It is unlikely that the younger generation of Mandinka jalis have the same profound knowledge of Sunjata as did Bamba Suso and Banna Kanute.

Of the two, Bamba Suso had the most direct links with Mali. His parents were from Galen, a village near the town of Kita in western Mali, the source of several major versions of Sunjata. Suso was considered an authority on Sunjata and other great heroes from Mande history, and he is still remembered today in the Gambia as one of the greatest Mandinka jalis of the century. Fortunately, we have Innes's text to provide concrete evidence of this, and its importance in the Sunjata tradition has been acknowledged by subsequent scholarship.

Although Bamba Suso had died by the time I (Lucy Durán) first did research in the Gambia in 1977, I knew well his accompanist, the virtuoso *kora* player Amadu Bansang Jebate. I also knew Banna Kanute. Knowing these two performers personally, and hearing them both perform on many different occasions, in the Gambia and in Europe, gave me much insight into the complexities of the jali tradition, and the difficulties that Innes (and other scholars) faced when trying to document a live performance on the printed page. My own experience also supported Innes's view that these musicians had very different personalities, and attitudes towards performance.

Bamba Suso, older than Banna Kanute by some twenty years, was not so much musician as oral historian, a 'master of the word'. His style of performance was quite matter-of-fact; for him clarity of speech was of paramount importance, more than the music itself. Suso only performed on very special occasions, for example, at a *sumungo* for private patrons. He rarely travelled, and he shunned the media.

Amadu 'Bansang' Jebate, the only musician of the three who is still alive, is now (1999) in his mid-eighties. A remarkable musician and story-teller in his own right, he frequently talked about his 'uncle' Bamba Suso, whom he had accompanied throughout his adult life. He had a number of copies of recordings of Suso made by Innes and Anthony King, which he was fond of listening to. These recordings were a springboard for Amadu to reflect on aspects of Suso's performance style, especially in so far as they reflected a Malian heritage. In the text presented here, Bamba Suso declares his Malian pedigree straight away, at the beginning of his performance of Sunjata. His father, Jali Musa Suso, was the first cousin of Amadu Jebate's father, Jali Fili Diabate. Both were from Galen, near Kita; both left Mali to settle in the Gambia under new patronage at the turn of the century. Bamba Suso's performance style is most definitely in this tradition.

In Kita and other centres of the Maninka tradition, senior male jalis – of fifty years or over – are no longer supposed to sing. The spoken voice is considered the most prestigious and effective 'mode' of performance, sometimes referred to as *tariku*, a localized version of the Arabic word meaning 'history'. When Bamba Suso spoke out his version of Sunjata for Innes, it was not because he could not sing, it was because he was obeying the Maninka dictates of how a jali of his status – a *ngara*, or 'master musician' – should perform. It is difficult to convey the quality of Suso's clear, booming, spoken voice, ringing out in perfect diction across the florid, staccato lines of Amadu Jebate's *kora*. Any Mandinka speaker can hear immediately, simply from the tone of voice, that this is a master jali, or *ngara*. His approach is straightforward, and didactic – he uses Sunjata to explain the origins of Mande surnames, social customs and even physical attributes (for example, the supposedly small wrists of the Darbo clan). Those who have heard performances by the late, great jali from Kita, Kele Monson Diabate, will recognize a similar 'no frills' style.

Though Banna Kanute was also from the upper-river area of the Gambia, he was a very different sort of musician. As Innes indicates, Banna had a powerful, flamboyant, sometimes abrasive personality, and was a born showman. A superb *balafon* player, he was given to abrupt and frequent changes in the accompaniment, moving restlessly from one tune to another, with a wide dynamic range, sometimes hitting the keys furiously hard, then so softly they could barely be heard. He would punctuate his singing with virtuosi instrumental interludes – ornamental flourishes up and down the keys of the *balafon* with lightning speed, while all the while he would hum along loudly. When narrating the Sunjata story, he would alternate between song and speech. He had a fine, strong singing voice, and, unlike Bamba Suso's clear, simple approach, Kanute's spoken words were delivered with considerable theatricality. All this emphasis on showmanship earned him some critics, who claimed he did not focus enough on the 'real' business of the jali, the story-telling.

In the 1950s, when few jalis travelled out of West Africa, Banna Kanute was already on the move, looking for broader opportunities as a musician. He spent some years in London in the 1950s, doing occasional recordings for the BBC World Service, and playing for London's burgeoning West African community (it was during this period that he made his recordings). After Gambia gained independence in 1965, Banna became one of the leaders of the Gambia National Troupe (the state-subsidized official ensemble of traditional musical instruments). The regimentation of a large ensemble did not, however, suit his temperament. In the later years of his life, he was performing mainly in the context of weddings and naming ceremonies, where songs such as Sunjata, with their ancient historical connections, had little place.

The story of Sunjata is an integral part of a Mande world-view. It serves to remind Mande peoples why they are who they are, and what behaviour is expected of them. On the broadest level, the name of Sunjata is a symbol of Mande cultural identity, and the name alone conjures up images of a glorious past, heroic behaviour, and moral values, that serve as a cultural matrix for Mande peoples. This is why, still today, every jali first learns to sing Sunjata's praise names, evoking his special relationship with his griots:

> Cats on the shoulder
> The hunter and the lion are at Naarena.

NOTES

1. Quoted in N. Levtzion, 'The early states of the Western Sudan to 1500', in J. F. Ade Ajayi and Michael Crowder (eds), *History of West Africa*, vol. 1 (London: 1976), 124.
2. Ibid., 125–6.
3. D. T. Niane, *Sundiata: an Epic of Old Mali* (London: 1965).
4. N. Levtzion and J. F. P. Hopkins, *Corpus of Early Arabic Sources for West African History* (Cambridge: 1981), 288–93.
5. Lucy Durán, 'Jelimusow: the superwomen of Malian music', in Graham Furniss and Liz Gunner (eds), *Power, Marginality and African Oral Literature* (Cambridge: 1995), 197–207.
6. Gordon Innes, *Sunjata: Three Mandinka Versions* (London: 1974), 15–20.
7. Ibid., 17.
8. D. C. Conrad, 'A town called Dakajalan: the Sunjata tradition and the question of ancient Mali's capital', *Journal of African History*, 35 (1994), 367.
9. See for example Johnson (1992).

A Note on the Text

This edition of the Sunjata epic is intended to introduce the general
reader to one of the greatest epic traditions of the African continent.
Widespread in the Mande-speaking areas of West Africa from the
Gambia to Guinea, across Mali and into Burkina Faso, the Sunjata epic
is a contemporary, living tradition rendered in countless versions, in a
wide variety of media. No single version captures the many different
stories that lie behind incidents and people that are woven into 'the
story'. This text is derived from a scholarly work, first published in
1974 by the School of Oriental and African Studies, London, in which
Gordon Innes, working with a collaborator Bakari Sidibe, translated
the texts of two performances of the epic given by the Gambian jalis
(griots), Bamba Suso and Banna Kanute. In the 1974 edition, entitled
Sunjata: Three Mandinka Versions, a third text by Dembo Kanute was
also included, but that text is not given here. Also in the 1974 edition
the full Mandinka texts were presented, along with extensive annota-
tion upon the language used. Further scholarly analysis was provided
of musical and performance aspects, including contributions from the
musicologist, Anthony King. The Mandinka texts and some of the
more detailed analysis have been omitted from the present volume.
The interested reader should refer to the 1974 edition for the complete
texts. The versions published in 1974 also contained sections where the
reciter addressed Innes and his collaborator Bakari Sidibe, as well as
passages which supplemented the narrative about Sunjata with further
information about some of his generals. These sections have been
omitted here (the places where they were are indicated by a line of
dots). We have also endeavoured to clarify some sections of the texts
by amending the translation on the basis of a re-reading of the Mandinka
transcripts, as well as by occasional amendment to the notes. Since the

1974 edition there has been substantial scholarly writing on the Sunjata epic, much of which is listed in the Further Reading.

As discussed in the Introduction, there are three modes of text and these are represented in this volume in the following manner: speech mode is presented as plain text, song in italics and recitation is given in semi-bold italics. The use of square brackets indicates translator or editorial additions, sometimes clarifying to whom the text refers. Round brackets mark asides by the performers.

Here and in the Further Reading and Explanatory Notes, the 'author-date' system (e.g. Johnson 1986) points to sources of information. Full bibliographic references are given at the end of the Further Reading.

The final 'e' in most Mande names is pronounced as in French 'é'. Anglophone orthographies do not use an accent, Francophone orthography does. Where a published author's name is presented with an accent we have retained it; otherwise the text uses the Gambian convention, as did the 1974 edition. There is further variety of spelling as the reader will discover.

To assist the general reader grasp the geography of the narrative, and the variety of ways by which reference is made to characters in the epic (different praise names, given names, family names), a map and two charts have been added to this edition; the charts give the names encountered in these texts, relating to Sunjata, his relatives and allies, and those of his arch-enemy Sumanguru. There are many other versions of the story in which these and other characters occur. For a detailed presentation of another set of characters and another chart of relationships see Johnson 1986 and 1992.

The editors would like to take this opportunity to thank those who have helped to bring this project to fruition: Gordon Innes, Martin Daly, Joy Hemmings-Lewis; and Anna South and Peter Carson both of Penguin Books. Without the original contributions by Bakari Sidibe, Bamba Suso, Amadu Jebate, Banna Kanute and Dembo Kanute, neither the 1974 edition nor this one would have existed. Our foremost thanks must in the end go to them.

Lucy Durán and Graham Furniss
School of Oriental and African Studies

Further Reading

Published transcriptions of performances of Sunjata include those of the celebrated Malian jalis (griots/bards) such as Kele Monson Diabaté from Kita (Bird 1972, Moser 1974, Diabaté 1975) and Fa-Digi Sisoko (Johnson 1986, 1992), Lansine Diabaté from Kela (Jansen et al., 1995) and Wa Kamissoko from Kirina (Cissé 1988, 1991). The last-named griot, who died in 1976, worked extensively with the Malian historian Youssouf Tata Cissé, whose two-volume work provides the most detailed documentation on Sunjata. This is part of a substantial body of academic scholarship on the subject of Mande griots (see for example Conrad and Frank 1995, Hoffman 1990) and Mande music (Charry 1992, Durán 1995). An extensive bibliographical essay covering various versions of Sunjata and secondary historical and literary studies is to be found in Johnson 1986. A new volume on Sunjata, edited by Ralph Austen (1999), contains a collection of essays by leading scholars who look at Sunjata as history, literature and performance. The volume includes essays on the genesis and history of Sunjata, on Sunjata in the wider world of West African epic, on Sunjata as written literature, and last, but certainly not least, on the cassette as means of transmission as well as 'intervention' in Mande epic recitations. The epic of Sunjata is one among a range of epic traditions from West and Central Africa. Extracts from some twenty-five such traditions are to be found in Johnson, Hale and Belcher 1997, with commentaries and a useful bibliography.

REFERENCES

Abrahamsson, H., *The Origin of Death: Studies in African Mythology* (Studia Ethnographica Uppsaliensia 11, Uppsala: 1951).

Austen, Ralph (ed.), *In Search of Sunjata: the Mande Oral Epic as History, Literature and Performance* (Indiana University Press, Bloomington: 1999).

Bird, Charles, 'Bambara oral prose and verse narratives collected by Charles Bird', in Richard M. Dorson (ed.), *African Folklore* (Anchor Books, New York: 1972).

Charry, Eric, *Musical thought, history and practice among the Mande of West Africa*, doctoral dissertation (University of Princeton, Princeton: 1992).

Cissé, Youssouf Tata and Wa Kamissoko, *La grande geste du Mali: des origines à la fondation de l'empire*, vol. 1 (Karthala, Paris: 1988).

Cissé, Youssouf Tata and Wa Kamissoko, *Soundjata: la gloire du Mali. La grande geste du Mali*, vol. 2 (Karthala, Paris: 1991).

Conrad, David C., 'A town called Dakajalan: the Sunjata tradition and the question of ancient Mali's capital', *Journal of African History*, 35 (1994).

Conrad, David and Barbara Frank (eds), *Status and Identity in West Africa: Nyamakalaw of Mande* (Indiana University Press, Bloomington: 1995).

Diabaté, Massa Makhan, *L'Aigle et l'épervier, ou la geste de Sunjata* (Éditions Pierre Jean Oswald, Paris: 1975).

Durán, Lucy, 'Jelimusow: the superwomen of Malian music', in Graham Furniss and Liz Gunner (eds), *Power, Marginality and African Oral Literature* (Cambridge University Press, Cambridge: 1995).

Hoffman, Barbara G., 'The power of speech: language and social status among Mande griots and nobles', doctoral dissertation (Indiana University, Bloomington: 1990).

Jansen, Jan, Esger Duintjer and Boubacar Tamboura, *L'Épopée de Sunjara, d'après Lansine Diabaté de Kela (Mali)* (Research School CNWS, Leiden: 1995).

Johnson, John William (with Fa-Digi Sisoko), *The Epic of Son-jara: a West African Tradition* (Indiana University Press, Bloomington: 1986, new edn 1992).

Johnson, John William, Thomas A. Hale and Stephen Belcher (eds), *Oral Epics from Africa: Vibrant Voices of a Vast Continent* (Indiana University Press, Bloomington: 1997).

Levtzion, Nehemiah, 'The early states of the Western Sudan to 1500', in J. F. Ade Ajayi and Michael Crowder (eds), *History of West Africa*, vol. 1 (Longman, London: 2nd edn 1976).

Levtzion, Nehemiah and J. F. P. Hopkins, *Corpus of Early Arabic Sources for West African History* (Cambridge University Press, Cambridge: 1981).

Moser, Rex, 'Foregrounding in the Sunjata, the Mande epic', doctoral dissertation (Indiana University, Bloomington: 1974).

Niane, D. T., 'Recherches sur l'empire du Mali au Moyen Age', *Recherches Africaines,* 1 (1960).

Niane, D. T., *Sundiata: an Epic of Old Mali*, translated by G. D. Pickett (Longman, London: 1965).

Pageard, Robert, 'Soundiata Keita et la tradition orale', *Présence Africaine*, 36 (1961).

Bamba Suso: Sunjata

It is I, Bamba Suso, who am talking,
Along with Amadu Jebate;
It is Amadu Jebate who is playing the *kora*,
And it is I, Bamba Suso, who am doing the talking.
Our home is at Sotuma;
That is where we both were born;
This tune that I am now playing,
I learned it from my father,
And he learned it from my grandfather.
10 Our grandfather's name – Koriyang Musa.
That Koriyang Musa
Went to Sanimentereng and spent a week there;
He met the jinns, and brought back a *kora*.
The very first *kora*
Was like a *simbingo*.
The *kora* came from the jinns.
Amadu Jebate's father's name was Griot Fili Jebate.
He came from Gaali in the East,
But the name of the area was Gaadugu.
20 My father, Griot Musa,
And Griot Fili were the sons of two sisters.
When my own father died it was Griot Fili who took my
    mother;
It was he whom I knew as my father.
All right,
I am going to tell you the story of Sunjata,
And you must pay attention.
Sunjata's father's name was Fata Kung Makhang.

He went to Sankarang Madiba Konte.
The soothsayers had said, 'If you go to Sankarang Madiba
   Konte
30 And find a wife there,
She will give birth to a child
Who will become king of the black people.'
He went there.
They had told him the name of this woman;
They called her Sukulung.
Nine Sukulungs were brought forward,
And a soothsayer consulted the omens,
And then declared, 'No, I do not see the woman among these
   ones.'
They said to Sankarang Madiba Konte,
40 'Now, is there not another Sukulung?'
He answered, 'There is, but she is ugly.
She is my daughter.'
He told him, 'Go and bring her here; I wish to see her.'
When they had brought her,
A soothsayer consulted the omens and then told him, 'This is
   the one.'
When Fata Kung Makhang had married her in Manding,
Then he and she went away.
She became pregnant, and for seven years
Sunjata's mother was pregnant with him.
50 She did not get a fright even once,
Except for one occasion.
Her husband called her,
During the rainy season, and he happened to speak at the same
   time that thunder sounded,
So that she did not hear him speak, and he repeated the call.
Then she went in trepidation to her husband.
That was the only fright that she ever got;
For seven years she never got a fright,
Except for that one occasion.
She gave birth to Sunjata.

60 The king had declared,
Fata Kung Makhang had declared, 'If any of my wives gives
    birth to a son,
I shall give my kingship to him.'
Sukulung Konte eventually gave birth –
Sunjata's mother.
They sent a slave, with the instructions, 'Go and tell Sunjata's
    father.'
At that time he had built a compound out on the farm land.
When the slave came he found them eating,
And they said to him, 'All right, sit down and have something
    to eat.'
The slave sat down.

70 It was not long before a co-wife of Sukulung's also gave birth.
When her co-wife gave birth, they sent a griot.
When the griot arrived he said, 'Greetings!'
They said to him, 'Come and have something to eat before
    you say anything.'
He said, 'No!'
The griot said, 'Naareng Daniyang Konnate,
Your wife has given birth – a boy.'
The slave was sitting; he said, 'They sent me first.
It was Sukulung Konte who gave birth first.'
Fata Kung Makhang declared,

80 'The one I heard of first,
He it is who is my son, the firstborn.'
That made Sunjata angry.
For seven years he crawled on all fours,
And refused to get up.
Those seven years had passed,
And the time had come for the boys who were to be
    circumcised to go into the circumcision hut.
People said, 'But Sunjata is crawling on all fours and has not
    got up;
The time to go into the circumcision hut has arrived, and all
    his brothers are going in.'

At that time they used to smelt ore and make iron from it;
90 The smiths put bellows to the ore,
And when they had smelted the ore they made it into iron,
And they forged the iron and made it into rods –
Two rods.
They put one into one of his hands,
And they put the other into his other hand,
And said that he must get up.
When he had grasped the rods, they both broke.
They said, 'How will Sunjata get up?'
He himself said to them, 'Call my mother;
When a child has fallen down, it is his mother who picks him
100   up.'
When his mother came,
He laid his hand upon his mother's shoulder,
And he arose and stood up.
It is from that incident that the griots say,
'The Lion has arisen,' they say, 'The Lion of Manding has
     arisen,
The mighty one has arisen.'
There were trousers in Manding;
Whoever was to be king of Manding,
If they put those trousers on you,
110 And you were able to get up with them on,
Then you would become king of Manding.
But if they put those trousers on you,
And you did not get up with them on,
Then you would not be king of Manding.
They brought those trousers,
But whichever of his brothers they put them on,
He was unable to get up with them on.
When they brought them to Sunjata,
They were trying to put them on Sunjata,
120 But the trousers did not fit Sunjata – they were too small –
Until a bit was added.
After that had happened they went into the circumcision shed.

After they had come out of there,
It was not long before his father died.
Sunjata announced, 'As for myself,
However extensive my father's property may be,
I want no part of it except the griots.'
They asked him, 'Do you want the griots?'
They said, 'Leave it;
A person who has nothing will not have griots for long.'
The griots said, 'Since he has let all his inheritance go,
And says that it is only us that he wants,
We will not abandon him.
If he does not die, we shall not desert him.'
The griots were at his side.
It happened that three things were distinctive in Sunjata's
        family:
They had three hairs on their body, and if you spoke the
        names of those hairs,
Whoever was a legitimate child would die that year.
The griots said, 'Ah, he has absolutely nothing,
So let us employ some guile and if he dies, then we can take it
        easy,
And go to men of substance.'
They went and begged from him.
When they went and begged from him,
He did not have anything.
He went and got honey in the bush,
And brought it back for the griots.
Whatever he gave them, they did not scorn it.
They went off; that is why the griots call him
**Bee, little bee, Makhara Makhang Konnate, Haimaru and
        Yammaru.**
Next morning they came and begged from him.
He had nothing,
So he went and caught a cat and gave it to them;
That is why the griots call him
Cats on the shoulder Simbong.

The griots came and begged from him again.
And he had nothing,
So he went and found some firewood in the bush and came
    back and gave it to them.
From that incident the griots say,
'Firewood Makhara Makhang Konnate, Haimaru and
    Yammaru,
160   *The lion is full of dignity, the resilient hunter.'*
The griots came and begged from him again.
He went and took a strip of cloth.
What he took was to the value of one shilling and sixpence.
It belonged to his brothers,
But no one dared to apprehend him
Because no one dared to stand up to him.
He gave it to the griots,
Who said, 'Jata has committed a theft';
It was that which gave him the name Sunjata;
170   His name was Makhang Konnate.
His name became Sunjata
When he took the one-and-sixpenny strip of cloth
And gave it to the griots.
They knew that he had taken it,
But no one dared to ask him about it.
The griots said, 'Jata has committed theft';
It was that which gave him the name Sunjata;
His name was Makhang Konnate,
Naareng Makhang Konnate –
180   That was his name.

Then that is how things were;
His brothers got together,
And then they went to a sorcerer
And told him, 'Attack him with *korte* till he dies.'
They gave a bull to the sorcerers.
They took this bull on to a hillside;
The sorcerers congregated,

Their leader was sitting;
One was saying, 'If I attack him in the morning, by evening he
    will be dead.'
190 Another was saying, 'If I attack him,
When he sees the roofs of the town, he will die.'
From that the Easterners say even today,
    'Home-person-taking.'
He himself was a hunter at that time.
He left the hunting area, having killed two elephants,
Whose tails he had in his hand.
He encountered the sorcerers on the hillside.
And he greeted them, but they did not answer him.
To the leader of the sorcerers he said,
'You ought to return my greeting.
200 When one freeborn person greets another,
He should return the greeting.
I have killed two elephants,
One of which is lying on the hillside.'
He took its tail out of his bag and threw it to them,
He said, 'I give it to you,
For you to add to your own meat.
But what you were sent to do,
Just do it!'
As he was about to go,
210 The leader of the sorcerers called him.
When he came, he said to him,
'You must leave Manding.
If someone says he will kill you,
A man's life is not in another man's hands,
But if he says he will ruin you,
Even if he does not ruin you, he could greatly hinder the
    fulfilment of your destiny,
It could be greatly delayed.'
Sunjata said, 'I cannot go,
My mother is at home.'
220 That was Sukulung Kutuma.

Hence the griots say, *'Sukulung Kutuma's child Sukulung*
    Yammaru,
Cats on the shoulder Simbong and Jata are at Naarena.'
Sunjata said, 'I cannot go;
My sister is at home.'
That was Nyakhaleng Jumo Suukho.
He said, 'My horn is at home,
My wine gourd is at home,
My bow is at home.'
The sorcerer said to him, 'I will summon all of them to the
    korte horn,
230 And they will answer the call.'
He called all of them to the *korte* horn and they answered the
    call.
He told Sunjata, 'Go!'
Sunjata's leaving Manding
And going to foreign lands came about in this manner.
On his way he came to a fork in the road,
He put down the *korte* horn and consulted it.
It told him, 'This road goes to Sankarang Madiba Konte,
This other road leads to Tamaga Jonding Keya' –
He was the ancestor of the Darbos.
240 Sunjata said, 'I shall go to Tamaga Jonding Keya's place,
Because if I go to the residence of my grandfather's sons,
My cousins and I are bound to end up quarrelling.'
He set off.
He reached Tamaga Jonding Keya's place,
And he found that they had put beeswax in a pot,
And the pot was boiling.
They took a ring and threw it into the hot wax,
And they were making their boasts on it.
This is what they were saying.
250 'If I am to become king of Manding,
When I plunge my hand into this boiling wax,
Let it not burn me.
But if I am not to be king of Manding,

When I plunge my hand into it,
Let my hand be destroyed.'
He found them making this declaration.
That was a public challenge.
Sunjata came and when he reached them,
He plunged his hand into that hot wax,
260 And took out the ring,
Threw it into cold water,
And gave it to Tamaga Jonding Keya.
Tamaga Jonding Keya was angry.
He said to Sunjata, 'There is a silk-cotton tree here;
If you are freeborn,
If you are legitimate –
We must go and shoot that silk-cotton tree.
Whoever misses that silk-cotton tree,
Whose arrow does not touch it,
270 Is not freeborn,
Is not legitimate.'
Sunjata was outraged
At the very thought that anyone should say to him in
     Manding,
'You are not legitimate.'
He went and drew his bow and shot the silk-cotton tree.
Tamaga Jonding Keya also drew his bow
And shot the silk-cotton tree.
Sunjata went and pulled out his arrow,
And said, 'If my mother was pregnant with me for seven years,
280 And she never had a fright,
Then when I shoot this silk-cotton tree, let it fall down.'
He shot the silk-cotton tree –
The tree remained standing.
He drew his knife,
He went and grabbed his mother's arm,
And said to her, 'Tell me about myself;
Tell me about the circumstances of my birth in Manding,
Otherwise I will kill you.'

Master of the lion! Master of the maga! *Master of the rhinoceros!*
290   *Ah, cats on the shoulder,*
Simbong and Jata are at Naarena.
Maabirama Konnate is no more.
Before Daniyang Konnate returned to the next world –
Naareng Daniyang Konnate has perished –
His griots were saying, 'Daniyang Konnate,
Are you afraid of death?'
He said, 'Death is not the thing I fear;
My griots must cross four great rivers,
They must cross four great swamps,
300   *They will come to a worthless man and an even more worthless one,*
And he will say, "Go away,
I swear I have nothing,
You are a griot,
You must get it from someone else.
Go away."'
He said, 'The dog was standing – may God lay him low,
When he is laid low, may God make him never rise again.'
Cats on the shoulder,
Simbong and Jata are at Naarena.
310   *The world does not belong to any man.*
Sunjata said to his mother,
'If I am a bastard,
Make it clear to me,
And I will kill you and kill myself.
If I am not a bastard in Manding,
Make it clear to me,
Because I shot the silk-cotton tree and it did not fall down,
And I had made my boast.'
She said to him, 'You went too far in your boast;
320   For seven years I was pregnant with you,
And I never had a fright,
But during the rainy season it was thundering,
And when your father called me I did not hear him,
And he called a second time.

That day I went in trepidation to your father.
Go and take that out of your boast and then see what happens.'
When he had removed that declaration from his boast,
He shot the silk-cotton tree,
And the tree leant over and was about to fall.
330 Tamaga Jonding Keya was standing nearby,
He shouted at the silk-cotton tree,
And the tree was about to rise up straight again,
Then Sunjata bellowed at the tree,
And it split down the middle and fell to the ground.
Even to this day when a silk-cotton tree is drying up,
It begins at the top,
It never dries up at the foot,
It begins at the top.
Tamaga Jonding Keya was angry,
340 And he boxed Sunjata's ear.
When he boxed Sunjata's ear,
Sunjata grabbed his arm and was about to cut his throat,
But Sunjata's sister came running up and stood beside him,
And said to him, 'When you were leaving Manding,
The soothsayers told you that you would have three causes for
    anger,
But that if you assuaged your anger by retaliating you would
    never be king of Manding.
This is one of those occasions for anger – leave it.'
That is why the wrists of the members of the Darbo family are
    not thick.
Tamaga Jonding Keya said to Sunjata, 'You are not going to
    remain here in my town,
350 Because anyone who is a greater man than I am
Will not remain here.'
Sunjata passed through that area
And went to Faring Burema Tunkara at Neema.
He stayed there; he was engaged in hunting,
He was engaged in hunting.

Of Sunjata's brothers who were installed as king [in
    Manding],
Any whom Susu Sumanguru did not kill by witchcraft,
He would kill in war.
If they made anyone king on Monday,
360 By the following Monday he would be dead,
Till all his brothers were finished,
And there remained only children.
Sunjata had a younger brother,
And they called him and told him, 'Go after your older
    brother;
His brothers are all finished,
The kingship has come to him.'
Sunjata's younger brother set off,
He kept on till he reached Neema.
When he reached Neema,
370 He was approaching it in the heat of the day.
He was quite exhausted when his sister caught sight of him.
One loves one's brother,
Especially after a long absence.
She ran to him
And had just taken hold of her brother,
When they both fell down.
He pushed her,
And his sister fell down.
Sunjata arrived,
380 Having just come from the bush,
And he saw his sister sitting with an unhappy look on her face,
And he asked her, 'What is the matter?'
She said, 'My brother pushed me and I fell down.'
Sunjata looked at his younger brother and he said to him, 'Fofana,
You will never be king of Manding.'
That was how the surname Fofana originated.
It happened that his mother was ill.
When Fofana had explained the reason for his journey, he said
    to Sunjata, 'Our brothers are all finished.

Susu Sumanguru has finished our brothers;
390   I was told to go for you,
So that you would come back;
The kingship of Manding has come to you.'
Sunjata stood by his mother's head
And said to her, 'Before dawn breaks tomorrow, if you die,
I am to be king of Manding.
As long as you remain ill,
I am not to be king of Manding,
Because I will not leave you here in illness.'
Before dawn broke, Sukulung Konte died.
400   Sunjata said that he would bury Sukulung Konte.
Faring Burema Tunkara told him,
'You will not bury her until you have bought the burial plot.'
Sunjata asked him, 'How am I to buy it?'
He said, 'You must fit earrings together,
And lay one upon her forehead,
And lay one upon her big toe,
And then measure the length on the ground;
However long the chain is, that is what you must dig,
And you will bury your mother there.'
410   When he had done that, he put the gold earrings together,
And he laid one upon his mother's forehead,
And he laid another upon her big toe,
And he measured it on the ground.
The gravediggers were about to go,
But he said to them, 'Wait!'
He took the gold and laid it on a new winnowing tray,
And he laid a broken pot on it,
He laid a bush fowl's egg on it,
He laid some old thatching grass on it,
420   And then he gave it to Faring Burema Tunkara.
When it had been given to Faring Burema Tunkara,
One of the latter's men was there who was called Makhang
    Know All,
And he declared, 'I know what this means.'

Makhang Say All was there;
Makhang Say All declared, 'But I will say it.'
Faring Burema Tunkara ordered him, 'Say it!'
He said, 'What Sunjata has said here
Is that a day will come
When he will smash this town of yours just like this broken pot;

430   A day will come
When old thatch will not be seen in this town of yours
Because he will burn it all;
A day will come
When bush fowls will lay their eggs on the site of your
     deserted town.
He says here is your gold.'
When he had done that, Sunjata buried his mother;
Then he and Nyakhaleng Juma Suukho,
And his younger brother,
And Bala Faaseega Kuyate

440   Rose up and went.
When he and Bala Faaseega Kuyate were on their way,
They had gone far into the bush,
And they had been travelling for a long time when Bala said, 'I
     am terribly hungry.'
Sunjata said, 'Wait here.'
He went into a clump of thick bush,
He examined the calf of his leg where there was plenty of flesh
     and he cut some off.
When he had cut it into thin strips, he cooked it,
Then he pounded the leaves of a medicinal shrub and then tied
     up his leg,
He applied *kuna fito* to the wound and tied it up.

450   He came back,
And he said to Bala, 'Here is some meat.'
He chewed the meat,
Had a drink,
And then said, 'Let's go.'
They went on for a long time;

When the wound turned septic, Sunjata was limping.
When Sunjata was limping,
Bala Faaseega Kuyate said to him,
'Naareng, why are you limping?'
460 Sunjata replied, 'Just let's go on.'
Bala said, 'I will not move from here until you tell me what
      the matter is.
Since the day I first met you,
I have never seen you
In the grip of such pain
That people were aware of it from your appearance;
But now you are limping.'
Sunjata said to him, 'You said you were hungry.'
He thrust his leg out of his gown,
And he told him, 'This is what I cut off and gave to you.'
470 There is a special relationship
Between the members of the Keita family and the members of
      the Kuyate family.
Even today, if a member of the Kuyate family deceives a
      member of the Keita family,
Things will go badly for him.
If a member of the Keita family deceives a member of the
      Kuyate family,
Things will go badly for him.

They carried on till they came to Dakhajala.
They stayed at Dakhajala.
Sunjata said to Bala Faaseega Kuyate,
'Haven't you called the horses for me?'
480 Bala asked, 'What sort of a thing is a horse?'
Sunjata said to him, 'A griot is an impatient fellow;
Just call the horses.'
Come horses! oh horses! mighty Sira Makhang,
A person who could argue with him.
Oh horses! mighty Sira Makhang,
Being dragged does not humiliate a great beast.

A long, long way through the bush, an outstanding stallion and a
        saddle,
Go quickly and come back quickly,
Giver of news from far away.
490   *A horse is something that goes far away,*
A horseman is someone who goes far away,
A horse is something that goes far away,
A horse's rein is something that goes far away,
A horse is something that goes far away,
A horseman is someone who goes far away.
A man who buys a horse never regrets it.
Ah, mighty war king,
A man who likes making deserted villages.
Many great matters have passed from the world.
500   *Ah, you have an army.*
You seize, you slay.
Maabirama Konnate, fighting goes well with you.
When he called the horses,
A white stallion appeared,
And Sunjata said, 'This is a fine-looking horse,
But if it falls ill, it will not recover.'
The griot called the horses,
And a brownish horse with white lower legs appeared,
And Sunjata said, 'I did not say this one.'
510   The griot called the horses,
A brownish horse with a white circle on its forehead
        appeared,
And Sunjata leapt on it first.
That is why the griots say,
'Oh horses, brownish horse.'
Sunjata told his griot, 'You must summon my leading men.'
Those who were known as leading men
Are what we Mandinka call army commanders,
And what the Easterners call men of death.
When he had summoned the leading men,
520   Kurang Karang Kama Fofana came –

A far-seeing man and a man who speaks with authority,
Kama crossed to the other side of the river with iron shoes,
Kama crossed the river with iron shoes.
He and one thousand,
Four hundred
And forty-four bowmen.
Sunjata declared, 'The time for battle has not yet arrived, Tira
    Makhang has not come.'
He told his griot, 'Call my leading men.'
Suru Bande Makhang Kamara came –

530   *Foobali Dumbe Kamara,*
    Makhang Koto Kamara, Manding Saara Jong,
    Jukuna Makhang Kamara, Baliya Kamara,
    Makhang Nyaame Kamara, Nyaani Saara Jong.
He too came with one thousand,
Four hundred and forty-four bowmen.
Sunjata told him, 'The time for battle has not yet arrived, Tira
    Makhang has not come.'
Sunjata said to his griot, 'Call the important men.'
He called them.
Sankarang Madiba Konte came –

540   *Sankarang Madiba Konte, Wuruwarang Kaaba and Dongeera,*
    Ganda who instils courage,
    Ganda who deprives of courage,
    Ganda, master of many arts.
    Faa Ganda killed his in-law on Monday,
    Next Monday Faa Ganda came into power;
    They say that you should not give your daughter to Faa Ganda,
    Killer of his in-law.
He and one thousand,
Four hundred,

550   And forty-
Four bowmen
Answered the call of Naareng Daniyang Konnate at Dakhajala.
Sunjata said to him, 'The time for fighting has not yet come,
    Tira Makhang has not come.'

Sankarang Madiba Konte demanded, 'Is Tira Makhang better
    than all the rest of us?'
Sunjata replied, 'He is not better than all the rest of you,
But he fights a morning battle,
He fights an evening battle,
And we join with him in the big battle.'
Sankarang Madiba Konte was Sunjata's grandfather;

560   He was angry, and he took out an arrow and fired it.
The arrow hit Muru,
It hit Murumuru,
It hit Gembe,
It hit Gembe's bold son,
It hit Seega, the Fula, in his navel.
That is why the griots say to members of the Konte family,
'Arrow on the navel Faa Ganda.'
They say if you see an arrow on a forehead,
It is Faa Ganda's arrow,

570   Because anyone who is shot in the forehead –
If anything has cut his head open –
Will not live.
Any serious illness which attacks you in the abdomen also
    never leaves you alive.
That is why they say, *'Arrow in the navel Faa Ganda,*
Arrow in the forehead Faa Ganda.'
They call him *Firer of the red arrow.*
He it was who shot the arrow
And slew Susu Sumanguru's father upon the hill.
All seven heads,

580   It was his arrow which smashed them all.
Sukulung Kutuma's child Sukulung Yammaru,
You are right, many great matters have passed,
Let us enjoy our time upon the earth.
A time for action, a time for speaking, a time for dying; knowing the
    world is not easy.
If you call a great man, no great man answers your call;
You must lay your hand upon the earth;

Many a great man is under the ground, a youthful king.

Had the ground a mouth, it would say, 'Many great men are under
   me.'

Maabirama Konnate, cats on the shoulder, Simbong and Jata are at
   Naarena,

590 *Your griots suffered when you were not there.*

Ah, you have an army,

You seize and you slay,

Sheikh 'Umar, man of war, war goes well for you.

(AMADU asks: At that time was Sunjata preparing to wage war
   against Susu Sumanguru?

BAMBA replies: He declared that he would not become king of
   Manding.

Until he and Susu Sumanguru had first joined battle.)

They were at that point

When Soora Musa came –

Kiliya Musa,

600 *Nooya Musa,*

Wanjagha Musa,

Bera Senuma,

Sangang Senuma,

Maadikani Senuma,

Konsikaya Koli Kumba, eye red as Bureng gold.

He too with one thousand, four hundred

And forty-four bowmen

Answered the call of Sunjata Konnate at Dakhajala.

Sunjata declared, 'The time for fighting has not yet come, Tira
   Makhang has not arrived.'

Soora Musa asked him, 'Naareng, is Tira Makhang better than
610 all the rest of us?'

Sunjata answered him, 'He is not better than all you others.

He fights a morning battle, he fights an evening battle,

Then we join with him in the big battle.'

(AMADU: Make clear to us which families, with which
   surnames,

Trace their descent from Tira Makhang.

BAMBA: When you hear the name Soora Musa,
If someone is called by the surname Dumbuya, that is Suuso.
If someone is called by the surname Kuruma, that is Suuso.
If someone is called by the surname Danjo, that is Suuso.
620   If someone is called by the surname Geyi, that is Suuso.
All of those are descended from Soora Musa.
If someone is called by the surname Njai, that is Konte.
If someone is called by the surname Jara, that is Konte.
When Tira Makhang rose up –
That Tira Makhang is the great Taraware.

. . . .

The Tarawares' surname is Tira Makhang.
The surname Dambele is Tira Makhang.
The surname Jebate is Tira Makhang.
630   The surname Job is Tira Makhang.
The surname Juf is Tira Makhang.
The surname Saane is Tira Makhang.
The surname Maane is Tira Makhang.
The descendants of Tira Makhang are all scattered,
Their surnames are all changed in this way,
But the original surname of all of them was Taraware.)
Tira Makhang was descended from Smoke,
Smoke fathered Flame,
Flame fathered Charcoal,
640   *Charcoal fathered Charcoal and Charcoal Chippings,*
And the latter fathered Tarakoto Bullai Taraware.
From that the griots say,
'Kirikisa the man who accompanies the king,
The man who rides horses to death and kills anyone who gainsays
  him.'
(AMADU: Then the warriors arrived.)
BAMBA: When Tira Makhang was coming,
He said, 'Wrap me in a shroud,
Because when I see Susu Sumanguru, either I put him in a
  shroud or he puts me in a shroud.
That is my declaration.'

650   He called his wives,
       And he put them in mourning,
       And he declared, 'When I see Susu Sumanguru,
       If he does not do this to my wives, then this is what I will do
          to his wives.'
       He then lay down upon a bier,
       And they carried it on their heads and came and laid it at
          Sunjata's feet,
       And Tira Makhang said to him, 'There is no need to make a
          speech;
       As you see me,
       When I see Susu Sumanguru,
       Either he will kill me and they will wrap me in a shroud and
          lay me upon a bier,
       Or else I will kill him and they will wrap him in a shroud and
660   lay him upon a bier.'
       (AMADU: At that time they were preparing for battle, but they
          had not yet set out.
       BAMBA: War had not yet broken out.
       At that time they were preparing for battle.)

       When the leading men had responded,
       The army rose up
       And battle was joined at Taumbaara.
       That day the fighting went well for the smith, Susu
          Sumanguru.
       They met next at Umbaara,
       And the fighting went well for Susu Sumanguru.
670   Then they met at Kankinyang.
       Susu Sumanguru took a bow
       And shot at Sunjata.
       When the arrows fell upon Sunjata's gown,
       He did this with his gown.
       The griots said to him, 'Are you afraid?'
       That is why the griots call him

Kubang Kubang Makhara Makhang Konnate Haimaru and
    Yammaru.

Sumanguru once shot at him with an arrow,

He dodged the arrow, and the griots said to him,

680   'Are you afraid of death, Naarena?'

It is from that incident that they call him *Dendending Makhara*
    Makhang Konnate,

Haimaru and Yammaru,

The lion is full of dignity, resilient hunter.

There was one occasion

When Sunjata walked very quickly,

And people thought that he was running away.

The griots said to him, 'Naareng, are you running away?'

The griots said to him, *'Kubang Kubang Makhara Makhang*
    Konnate,

Haimara and Yammaru,

690   *The lion is full of dignity, resilient hunter;*

If a lion had not broken his bones, a fool's wife would not be in need
    of strength.'

Fighting went on till the sun had set,

When it was evening, Sunjata's sister came to him –
    Nyakhaleng Juma Suukho –

And said, 'To be sure, hot water kills a man,

But cold water too kills a man.

Leave the smith and me together.'

She was the best-looking woman in both Susu and Manding.

When she had got herself ready,

She left the land of Manding and went to the land of Susu.

700   When the woman had gone some distance she reached Susu,

She reached Susu Sumanguru.

The gates of his fortified town –

The griots call smiths

Big kuku Tree,

Big Silk-cotton Tree,

Push-in-front Expert,

And Lift the Hammer.

Those were the names of the gateways of the fort,
They were gateways with porches.
710 Whenever the woman reached a gateway,
When she knocked, the guards would ask her,
'Where are you going?';
Inevitably they were all smitten with love for her,
But she would tell them, 'I am not your guest;
I am the guest of Susu Sumanguru.'
She would go and knock at another door,
Till she had passed through all the doorways.
They took her to Susu Sumanguru.
When Susu Sumanguru saw her,
720 He greatly desired the woman.
He welcomed her to the house,
And gave her every kind of hospitality.
Night fell,
And he and the woman were in his house.
Now, a princess of Manding
And a smith would not sleep together.
They were chatting,
Till the smith's mind turned in a certain direction,
And then she said to him, 'I am a guest;
730 I have come to you –
Don't be impatient.'
She said to him, 'There is something that greatly puzzles me;
Any army which comes to this town of yours is destroyed.'
Susu Sumanguru said to her,
'Ah, my father was a jinn.'
When he said that, his mother heard it,
Because Susu Sumanguru's
Mother was a human being,
But his father was a jinn.
740 Two women had conceived him;
As you may know, the griots praise smiths in terms of this,
Saying, *'Between Susuo and Dabi, take suck from two mothers.'*
Two women had conceived him;

When he was inside one of them,
She was fit, and people saw her going about
For a week or ten days, and the other one was ill;
When he returned to the other one,
The one he came out of became ill.
He would return inside her
750   For a week or ten days and people saw her around too.
That is why they called him *Between Susuo and Dabi, take suck from two mothers.*
But when these events were taking place,
Dabi was still alive.
When Sumanguru said to Sunjata's sister, 'My father is a jinn,'
The old lady appeared,
And said to him, 'Don't give away all your secrets to a
    one-night woman.'
When Susu Sumanguru's mother said that, the woman got up
    and said to him,
'I'm going, because your mother is driving me away.'
He said, 'Wait!'
760   He went and gave his mother some palm wine,
And she drank it, became drunk and fell asleep.
He said to Sunjata's sister, 'Let us continue with our chat.
She is an old lady.'
They were chatting,
And she said to him, 'Did you say that your father is a jinn?'
He said, 'My father is a jinn, and he lives on this hill.
This jinn has seven heads.
So long as he is alive, war will never damage this country.'
She said to him, 'Your father,
770   How can he be killed?'
He said, 'You must go and find a white chicken,
Then they must remove the spur of the white chicken,
They must pick the leaves of self-seeded guinea-corn,
They must put *korte* powder in it.
If they put that on the tip of an arrow,
  And shoot it at this hill,

They will kill my father.

That is the only thing that will kill him.'

She asked him, 'Supposing they kill him?'

780   He replied, 'If war came, this country would be destroyed.'

She asked, 'Supposing this land were destroyed, what would
        happen to you?'

He said, 'I would become a whirlwind.'

She said, 'Supposing people went into the whirlwind with
        swords?'

He said, 'I would become an African fan-palm.'

She said to him, 'What if people were about to fell the palm?'

He said, 'I would become an ant-hill.'

She asked, 'Supposing people were about to scatter the
        ant-hill?'

He said, 'I would become a Senegalese cou–'

His heart palpitated,

790   And he fell silent.

The woman said to him, 'Wait,

I am going to the wash–place,

Because a woman and a man do not go to bed together dirty.'

(AMADU: That 'Senegalese cou–' – what was it he cut short
        there?

BAMBA: He had cut short the name 'Senegalese coucal'.

Even today, if you fire at a Senegalese coucal in the bush,

Quite often the gun will shatter in your hands.)

Nyakhaleng Juma was in the wash–place,

And Susu Sumanguru was in bed inside the house.

800   After some time, he would say to her,

'Aren't you coming back today?'

At that time in Manding

They had a *korte* ring,

And when they laid it down,

And the person for whom it had been laid down spoke,

It would answer him.

It did not answer everybody,

But it would answer the person for whom it had been laid
    down.
She took off that *korte* ring
810   And threw it into the pot of ablution water.
When Sumanguru said, 'Aren't you coming?'
It would say to him, 'Wait;
Such is this fort of yours
That a guest who comes to you
Is completely in your hands.
You are king;
Why are you so impatient?'
When she had thrown the ring in there,
She climbed over the wall of the fort and off she went.
820   When she had gone, Sumanguru lay for a long time,
He had a short nap,
Then he awoke with a start
And went and looked inside the wash-place.
He said, 'I think there is more to this than just a visit to the
    wash-place.'
He did not find anyone there.
At length he came upon the *korte* ring,
But he did not see anyone.
He wept.
She reached Sunjata,
830   And she told him all that Sumanguru had said.
They went and found a white cock,
They found self-seeded guinea-corn,
They found *korte* powder.
That is why the members of the Kante family do not eat white
    chicken.
When they had prepared this arrow,
They gave it to Sankarang Madiba Konte.
It was Sankarang Madiba Konte who fired the arrow.
That is why the griots say, *'The head and neck of an arrow both
    with red* **mananda**,
Arrow on the forehead Faa Ganda.'

It was he who slew the jinn on the hill [Susu Sumanguru's
840   father].
When he had slain the jinn on the hill in Susu,
The griots called him *The red arrow firer of Manding.*
Next morning the army rose up and flung itself against the
        fortified town;
It was not yet two o'clock when they smashed it.
Nyakhaleng Juma Suukho was with the army,
Since the soldiers were searching for Sumanguru.
When the head of a snake is cut off,
What remains is just a piece of rope.
They were searching for the king;
They were engaged on that, when she saw a great whirlwind
850   arise,
And she shouted to them, 'That's him, don't let him get away!'
They rushed upon that whirlwind,
Armed men were entering it, when they saw a fan-palm
        standing.
She said to them, 'This is him!'
They rushed, and were about to fell the palm tree,
When he changed into an ant-hill.
She shouted to them, 'This is him!'
They took axes and were just about to smash the ant-hill to
        pieces,
When they saw a Senegalese coucal fly up
860   And go into an area of thick bush.
Manda Kante,
Saamagha Kante,
Tunkang Kante,
Baayang Kante,
Sege and Sirimang,
It is forging and the left hand,
Between Susuo and Dabi,
Frustrater of plots.
It went into thick bush.
870   This was how Susu Sumanguru's career ended.

That is where my own knowledge ends.
Then Sunjata took control of Susu and Manding.
The mode of life of people at that time
And our mode of life at the present day are not the same.
Surnames did not exist.
All the surnames with which we are familiar
Were given by Sunjata,
Because he was an extraordinary person.
If you had done anything noteworthy,
880   Then, when you appeared before him,
He would greet you with a name related to that.
At that time these Danso surnames –
There is an animal in the East,
Which is there even today, and which they call *dango*.
That *dango* denied people passage along the road;
People did not pass that way.
It was a rhinoceros: what we Westerners call a rhinoceros,
And which the Easterners call *dango*.
The ancestor of the Damfas killed that creature;
890   When he came to Sunjata, the latter called him Damfagha.
That was the origin of the surname Damfa.
The ancestor of the Dansos – a snake was lying across the road,
No one passed by that way.
The road from east to west was cut,
And it was that snake which had cut it.
The ancestor of the Dansos killed that snake;
When he came, Sunjata said to him, *'Kenyeramatigi,*
    road-clearing lion.'
He added, 'It was you who opened up the road.'
He said to him, *'Road-clearing lion.'*
Even today the Mandinka say, 'So-and-so has cleared the road
900   in front of us.'
That was he,
That was the ancestor of the Dansos.
When Sunjata had taken over the kingship,
He told Tamaga Jonding Keya, 'Darbo,

You must give up your interest in the kingship of Manding
    now.'
As you know, they call the members of the Suso family *Red
    Bureng Gold*.
Soora Musa [Faa Koli] had been king of Manding,
And when Sunjata became king,
The old king and the new king did not trust one another.

910   Soora Musa gave Sunjata a great quantity of gold.
At Tabaski, Sunjata said to him, *'Eye red as Bureng gold.'*
That was Soora Musa.
When they had killed Susu Sumanguru,
Sunjata became master of both countries.
He did not have any enemies,
He did not have any rivals.
Susu and Manding both belonged to Sunjata,
And his reign endured for a long time.

Banna Kanute: Sunjata

In this account which I give,
And which opens here,
The subject which I am going to talk about
Is the career of Makhang Sunjata,
As I have heard it,
Because the Sunjata story
Is very strange and wonderful.
You see one griot,
And he gives you an account of it one way,
And you will find that that is the way he heard it;
You see another griot,
And he gives you an account of it in another way,
And you will find that what he has heard has determined his
   version.
What I have myself heard,
What I have heard from my parents,
That is the account which I shall put before you.
Sunjata's mother's name was Sukulung Konte.
Sukulung Konte,
Her father was Sankarang Madiba Konte.
Sankarang Madiba Konte,
He was a great king.
That king,
Sankarang Madiba Konte, was descended from Khulubu Konte;
Khulubu Konte,
It was he who begat Khulubu Khalaba Konte.
Sankarang Khulubu Konte and Khulubu Khalaba Konte –
It was Dala Kumbukamba who was the father of Dala Jiibaa
   Minna;

Dala Jiibaa Minna was the father of Kasawura Konte;
It was Kasawura Konte who was the ancestor of Sunjata,
30   As I have heard it.

In the reign of Dugu and Bala, Faabaga and Taulajo,
Sunjata's mother, Sukulung Konte, was that king's sister.
Sunjata's father,
Naareng Makhang Konnate,
In their section of the town,
He fathered twelve sons.
Naareng Sira
Was the father of Naareng Makhang,
Naareng Makhang was the father of Makhang Konnate,
40   Makhang Konnate was the father of Makhang Sunjata.
Before Sunjata was born,
As I have heard it from the traditional narrators,
His mother had had twenty pregnancies by his father –
Forty sons.
At that time Mansa Farang Tunkara
Was reigning, the ancestor of the Tunkaras,
But he was not within the town of Manding.
It was the head of the smiths, Susu Sumanguru Baamagana,
Who was at that time reigning in Manding.
50   There were twelve sections in Manding;
The Jaanes had a section there,
The Kommas had a section there,
The Tures had a section there,
The Siises had a section there.
All of these were within the town of Manding,
But they were not in control of the town,
They did not seek the kingship;
They had their Islamic faith.
Dugu and Bala,
60   *Faabaga and Taulajo,*
Supreme horseman whom none surpasses.

Susu Sumanguru Baamagana, the ancestor of the smiths,
He it was who was at that time the king of Manding.
They used to quarry iron ore and smelt it and make iron from
    it and forge it.
They made guns with it,
And they made bullets with it.
He used to make his own gunpowder;
He it was who was in control of the town of Manding.
In his time
70 A tall, slender baobab tree grew within the town of Manding.
This little baobab tree was round; it grew up,
And produced a single fruit.
When you say 'one single fruit',
That means that it produced one fruit.
As to that fruit, all the marabouts declared it,
All the diviners by cowries declared it,
All the diviners by stones declared it,
The diviners by sand declared it,
They predicted that whoever swallowed a single seed of the
    fruit of that baobab
80 Would be in control of the town of Manding for sixty years.
Before Sunjata was born,
The forty sons whom his father had begot
Had perished in the Prophet's war at Haibara.
Then in the days of the Prophet Muhammad,
That too was the time of Sunjata's father.
Those forty sons became soldiers of the Prophet;
They went to the war at Haibara, where they perished.
It befell that the Prophet
Sent Sorakhata Bunjafar to Sunjata's father,
90 With the message, 'You must give me soldiers;
I am going to wage war upon the infidels at Haibara.'
Sorakhata came and stood by Sunjata's father
And said to him, 'The handsome Slave of God says that you
    must give him soldiers;
They are going to fight at Haibara.'

Sunjata's father called Sunjata's mother, Sukulung Konte,
And he said to her,
'The Messenger of God has sent this man here;
He says that I must give him fighting men,
Because he is going to wage war at Haibara.'
100   He summoned his wife to speak.
His wife said to him, 'From the time that I married you
Up to this year – how many years does that make?'
He told her the number of years.
She said to him, 'Have I ever gainsaid you?'
He answered, 'No.'
'Have I ever refused you anything?'
He answered, 'No.'
She said to him, 'I serve you,
I serve God,
110   When you say what should be done,
Am I to argue with you about it?'
He gave his forty sons to Sorakhata Bunjafar,
And they went off to the Prophet's war at Haibara, where they
        perished.
When God's Messenger withdrew from the Haibara war,
Then the war was over.
Sukulung Kutuma,
And Sukulung Yammaru,
Naareng Makhang Konnate,
Cats on the shoulder,
120   *Simbong and Jata are at Naarena.*
When the Prophet had returned home he summoned
        Sorakhata
And said to him, 'Sorakhata, go and tell Makhang Konnate
That his forty sons have perished.'
At that time Sunjata's mother was old;
For a long time she and Sunjata's father had not lived in the
        same house,
For a period of some twelve years in fact.
They just cooked lunch for the two of them,

They used to eat and sit together in the same place and
   converse with each other,
But his mother had passed the age
130   Of going into the husband's house.
This tune which I am playing
Is one which was played to Sunjata in Manding.
This tune was played to Faa Koli Kumba and Faa Koli Daaba.
He was a fierce warrior of Sunjata's.
He was descended from the ancestor of the Sooras,
Kiliya Musa and Nooya Musa,
Bula Wuruwuru and Bula Wanjaga,
Futu Yokhobila and Sina Yokhobila,
Bumba Yokhobila;
140   He had a spear
Which was called *Tuluku Muluku,*
One place where it enters, nine places where blood comes forth.
If it pierced your body in one place,
Blood would issue forth in nine places.
That is why he was called Soora: Piercer;
In the eastern dialect they call him 'Soora'.
Sorakhata arrived,
He came and stood by Makhang Konnate,
And he said to him, '*Dugu and Bala,*
150   *Faabaga and Taulajo,*
Supreme horseman whom none surpasses,
Wuruwarang Kaba,
Dala Kumbukamba,
And Dala Jiibaa Minna,
Kasawura Konte,
Dugu and Bala,
Faabaga and Taulajo,
Supreme horseman whom none surpasses.'
He said, '*Sukulung Kutuma,*
160   *And Sukulung Yammaru,*
Naareng Makhang Konnate,
Cats on the shoulder,

Simbong and Jata are at Naarena.'
He said to him, 'God's Messenger declared that I should tell
    you
That all your forty sons have perished at Haibara.'
Makhang Konnate leapt up and shouted, 'Praise be to God,
    Master of the worlds,
I shall give thanks to the Lord who created me;
Even though I myself have done no service for God which
    would take me to Paradise
Those forty sons of mine,
170   Whom I got in honourable wedlock –
I believe that the Holy War in which they died
Will save my wife and myself in the next world.'
Sorakhata returned
And delivered this report to God's Messenger;
God's Messenger went into retreat at night
And performed twelve *rak'a*.
He begged God
To send down good fortune upon Sunjata's mother and father,
And to provide them with means of support.
180   After that, God in His omnipotence
Returned Sunjata's mother to what she had been as a young
    woman.
Her flesh did not change,
But she reverted to a fourteen-year-old girl.
She approached Sunjata's father
And she became pregnant with Sunjata.
At that time Sunjata's sister was there;
She was called Nene Faamaga.
At that time the leader of the smiths was king of Manding.
That baobab tree which grew within the town of Manding
190   Had had dry wood piled up round it.
It was announced that when the fruit of the baobab fell,
One person from each section of the town should get some
    and eat it,
Since, as to that baobab tree,

The marabouts had declared,
And the diviners by cowries had likewise declared,
That whoever ate one seed of that baobab tree
Would be in control of the town of Manding for sixty years.
After Sunjata's mother had become pregnant,
In the seventh month of her pregnancy, Sunjata's father died.
200 Only she and Sunjata's sister were left.
His mother was left with nothing.
Except a cow and its calf and one cat and one dog.
That cow was in the herd,
Together with its one calf;
When they had fetched the milk,
Sunjata's mother used to curdle it,
And when she had exchanged the curdled milk for millet,
She would pound the millet,
She would put the flour in a steamer,
210 And that, with the little drop of milk left over,
Was what she and Sunjata's sister lived on.
Sunjata was not yet born.

Kiliya Musa and Nooya Musa,
Bula Wuruwuru and Bula Wanjaga,
Futu Yokhobila, Sina Yokhobila, Karata Kobila,
Bagala Nyankang Musa and Fitaga Musa,
Bula Banna Jajura.
The drums which were used to summon an assembly sounded
    for his grandfather,
Great Bagadugu and Ginate,
220 *Great Hanjulu and Hanunayanga,*
They say that Faa Koli Kumba had a spear and a bow,
Faa Koli Daaba,
At that time he was in Manding.
It was Jinna Musa who was his father.

Of Sunjata's mother,
People used to say,

'Is this woman pregnant,
Or is she ill, or has she been poisoned?'
After it had happened,
230   That Sunjata's mother had become pregnant,
When she had been pregnant for one year,
Susu Sumanguru Baamagana's diviners by stones said to him,
'The child who will destroy your kingship
Has been conceived within Manding.'
Sumanguru gathered together all the women of the town of
     Manding,
And for seven years
He kept them within a walled town.
A man and a woman did not lie on the same bed,
A man and a woman did not come near each other.
240   As for those women who did become pregnant,
If they gave birth to a child and that child was a male,
Its throat was cut – for seven years.
When it became known that Sunjata had been conceived,
The griots composed this song:
Ah, it is of Jata that I speak, great stock,
Simbong, it is of Jata that I speak, great stock destined for high office.
In those seven years,
Any woman who became pregnant in Manding
Was taken inside that walled town,
250   And this went on for fourteen years.
For fourteen years
Sunjata's mother was pregnant with him,
But the diviners by stones foretold it,
The diviners by cowries foretold it;
They told Susu Sumanguru Baamagana,
'The child who will destroy your kingship
Has already been conceived.'
Sukulung Kutuma,
And Sukulung Yammaru,
260   *Naareng Makhang Konnate,*
Cats on the shoulder,

Simbong and Jata are at Naarena.
As to Sunjata's reputed running away,
The griots made a fine name out of it.
Susu Sumanguru Baamagana went to the leader of the Siises,
And sent him into retreat for forty days.
This child who was to destroy his kingship –
Had he been born yet?
Or had he not?

270 Was he in Manding?
These were the questions he must answer.
He must devise some strategy
So that he can work magic against the child and so be able to
    kill him.
The leader of the Siises went into retreat;
He came out,
And he found Susu Sumanguru Baamagana –
Cut and Sirimang,
It is forging and the left hand,
Senegalese coucal and swallow,

280 *Cut iron with iron,*
What gives iron its excellence,
Big kuku *tree and big silk-cotton tree,*
Fari and Kaunju –
He was sitting.
He told Sumanguru, 'I went into retreat
For forty days;
I saw the seven layers of the sky,
Right to where they finish;
I saw the seven layers of the earth,

290 Right to where they finish;
I saw a black thing in a pond;
By the grace of God,
The creature which comes and gives me information in the night
Came and stood beside me and said,
"Allahu aharu rajaku fa mang kaana kaafa,
Ming muusi, janafang kumfai kuna."

God declares that by his grace,
Whomsoever he has created king,
He has made his own likeness,
300   And nothing will be able to injure that person.
Those things which you must enjoy,
Enjoy them now, before this child is born,
For after he is born,
You will be powerless against him.
If you do not believe that,
You should release two white cocks within your compound,
And name one of them after yourself,
And one after this child.
Since you do not know his name,
310   You must mark it in some way;
You must fashion pure gold
And put it on your namesake's leg,
And you must fashion pure silver
And put it on the leg of the child's one.'
Sukulung Kutuma
And Sukulung Yammaru,
Naareng Makhang Konnate,
Cats on the shoulder,
Simbong and Jata are at Naarena.
320   *In Sunjata's day a griot did not have to fetch water,*
To say nothing of farming and collecting firewood.
Father World has changed, changed.
Almighty God, my thoughts here go to
Makhang Sunjata, a wonderful episode.
Sumanguru kept those two white cocks in his compound.
A day came
When Susu Sumanguru Baamagana
And his griots were sitting,
Along with his smiths
330   And his attendants.
At that time Bala Faasigi Kuyate belonged to Susu Sumanguru
    Baamagana.

A marabout arrived;
Sumanguru was sitting;
Bala Faasigi Kuyate said,
'Cut and Sirimang,
It is forging and the left hand,
Senegalese coucal and swallow,
Cut iron with iron,
What makes iron valuable,
340 *Big kuku tree and big silk-cotton tree,*
Fari and Kaunju.'
The chicken named after Sunjata crowed.
When the one named after Sunjata crowed,
The one named after Susu Sumanguru Baamagana also
   crowed.
When the one named after Sumanguru crowed,
The one named after Sunjata attacked it.
They seized hold of each other,
And fought,
And fought,
350 And fought,
Till the one named after Sumanguru turned tail
And ran under the leg of Sumanguru's chair.
The one named after Sunjata seized it by the comb
And pulled it out
And shook it;
It opened its mouth,
And saliva dribbled out.
The griot, Bala Faasigi Kuyate, was sitting.
Susu Sumanguru Baamagana ordered,
360 'Go and catch that chicken and destroy it;
Don't let it die a natural death.'
They seized it and slaughtered it.
The marabout was sitting;
He said, 'Susu Sumanguru Baamagana,
I went into retreat –
Is this the votive offering which I prescribed for you?'

Sumanguru said, 'Yes.'

The marabout asked, 'Did you see what one chicken did to the
    other?

If you touch this child,

370   That is what he will do to you.'

(As you may know, the members of the Kante family do not
    eat white chicken,

And the reason for this is

That when Sunjata and Susu Sumanguru met,

It was a white chicken which killed the latter.

As to the white chicken which killed him,

They took the spur of a white cock

And they put gold dust and silver dust inside it,

And that is what they eventually killed Susu Sumanguru
    Baamagana with.

After Sunjata had captured them,

380   He changed the smiths' surname;

He made their surname Kante.

As regards all those in Manding,

That is the reason that the members of the Kante family do not
    eat white chicken.

I shall come to that in due course,

And I shall tell you about that when I come to it.)

. . . .

Susu Sumanguru Baamagana was perplexed;

He lay down for the night.

All this time Sunjata's mother was pregnant with him.

All this took place in those twelve years.

Sumanguru went to the leader of the Jaanes

And took him to his compound,

410   Where they sat together;

He said, 'Bala Faasigi Kuyate!',

And the latter answered;

Sumanguru went on, 'I summoned the leader of the Siises,

And told him to divine by dreams

And to divine also by other techniques

So that he could devise some stratagem against the child who,
      it is said,
Will be born in Manding,
And who will destroy my kingship –
Some stratagem so that he could work against the child on my
      behalf
420   And destroy him for me
Before he comes to anything.
He went into retreat;
After forty days he came out.
He prescribed two white chickens as a votive offering;
I kept those two white chickens in my compound.
Of those two white chickens,
The one named after the child killed the one named after me.
I have called upon the leader of the Jaanes
To work for me,
430   And to investigate how things stand for me,
And to see if he can do anything.'
Sukulung Kutuma
And Sukulung Yammaru,
Naareng Makhang Konnate,
Cats on the shoulder,
Simbong and Jaata are at Naarena.
The leader of the Jaanes replied, 'All right, I have heard.'
He too went off;
He went into retreat;
440   After forty days he came out.
That is why,
Among us black people,
A white cock is prescribed as a votive offering,
For every boy.
Afterwards, when you grow up and build your own
      compound,
A white ram is prescribed as an offering by you.
As to the origin of this custom,
This is how it came about.

He too went into retreat;
450   After forty days he came out.
He came and said to Susu Sumanguru Baamagana,
'I have seen the seven layers of the sky,
Right to where they end;
I have seen the seven layers of the earth,
Right to where they end;
The creature which often stands beside me
Came and stood beside me,
A spirit in human form,
And it said to me, "Hata nuta
460   Muslama utiya rusululai
Wollahi alamu."
It said that a created thing will not know God.
God declared that he had ordained this and it could not be
    altered.
But if you do not believe it,
You must give two white rams as a votive offering.
You must name one of them after yourself,
And the name of the person whom you fear,
That person whom God will make manifest,
His name must you give to the other ram.
470   You must watch those two white rams,
Because what happens with them
Will, if you touch this child,
Happen also with the two of you.'
All this time Sunjata's mother was pregnant with him.
He had a sister, Nene Faamaga,
Who was in love with a spirit king.
That spirit king
Lived in a hill called Yura.
The spirit king's name was Manga.
480   You must have noticed among the griots
A tune which they play called 'Manga Yira';
It is not strictly 'Manga Yira', it is 'Manga Yura'.
Every Monday night

Sunjata's sister would go and sleep with that spirit king, Manga
    Yura.
In the Yalunka language, when you hear the word *mangga*,
That means 'king';
Yura means 'hill'.
That hill, Yura, stood on the outskirts of the town of
    Manding.
Every Monday night
490 Nene Faamaga would go and sleep with the spirit king there.
Every Friday night
She would go and sleep with the spirit king,
And he would say to her, 'This pregnancy of your mother's –
The child she is to bear will become a king;
His name will be Sunjata.'
The leader of the Jaanes
Prescribed these two white rams
For Susu Sumanguru Baamagana.
Cut and Sirimang,
500 *It is forging and the left hand,*
Senegalese coucal and swallow,
Cut iron with iron,
What makes iron valuable,
Big kuku *tree and big silk-cotton tree,*
Fari and Kaunju;
The smith who brings out the koma *masquerader is leading the*
    smiths,
Fataga Magaso is leading the smiths.
Don't you see,
Susu Sumanguru Baamagana is cold;
510 *Their day is past.*
Sumanguru kept the two white rams in his compound.
He fashioned pure silver
And attached it to the leg of the one named after himself;
He intended to change matters.
He fashioned pure gold
And attached it to the one he had named after Sunjata.

Since he did not know Sunjata's name
He said, 'The person whom God is to create,
Is he not yet born?
520 Is he in this town?
Is he in his mother's womb?
Is he a spirit?
If it be God's will,
It is that child who will destroy my reign;
It is after him that I name this ram.'
He put the pure gold on that one.
Those two white rams were together for some time,
Then a day came,
Susu Sumanguru Baamagana –
530 It was the evening before Friday;
Thursday was nearly over and the evening before Friday had
        begun,
When dawn broke it would be Friday –
Susu Sumanguru Baamagana and his attendants were sitting;
The sheep appeared,
With the two white rams among them;
The one named after Sunjata mounted a ewe
And was about to couple with it;
The one named after Sumanguru took a few steps backwards
And butted the one named after Sunjata.
540 The latter left the ewe
And faced the other ram.
They butted each other,
And butted each other,
And butted each other,
Susu Sumanguru Baamagana was sitting
With his griots
And his attendants.
The ram named after Susu Sumanguru Baamagana
Pulled back a little way,
550 Sunjata's namesake did likewise;
As they crashed into each other,

One of the horns of Susu Sumanguru Baamagana's namesake
    snapped.
Sunjata's namesake pulled back a little way,
Then came crashing into the other ram,
Which fell to the ground.
The attendants fell upon it and slaughtered it.
Sumanguru was perplexed;
He went to the leader of the Jaanes,
And told him what had happened.
560   The leader of the Jaanes said to him,
'I am not God,
But since I began serving God,
Since I first knew my right hand from my left,
On any occasion when someone gave me work to do,
I went into retreat,
And what I saw, I saw;
That is what I have seen in this instance.
That is what the Lord has revealed to me.
He declares that he is God and that no one can know him.
570   He has ordained this kingship and it cannot be altered.
Therefore enjoy such luck as you are going to enjoy
Before this child appears.'
. . . .

580   Sumanguru went to the leader of the Kommas.
When he had summoned the leader of the Kommas,
The latter came.
Susu Sumanguru Baamagana said to him,
'Leader of the Kommas,
I summoned the leader of the Siises
And I set him to work on this matter;
He went into retreat,
And after forty days he came out,
And he prescribed a chicken as a votive offering – two white
    chickens.
590   I kept two white chickens in my compound,
And when I did that,

The namesake of the person I am afraid of
Killed my namesake.
Then I went to the leader of the Jaanes,
And I set him to work on this same matter.
He too went into retreat,
For forty days;
He prescribed two rams for me as an offering.
The child's namesake killed my namesake.

600 I have come to you, leader of the Kommas,
To help me,
So that, as far as this child is concerned,
Even if I cannot kill him,
At least I may remain king,
And no one may drive me from the kingship.'
The leader of the Kommas went into retreat, then came out,
And he said to Sumanguru, 'Until three years have elapsed I
    shall not be able to work against him.'
Within that time Sunjata was born;
He was a male child.

610 His mother went to the wash-place
And there she dug a hole
Into which she put Sunjata.
Then she put a steamer on top of him
So that he could breathe,
For she was afraid.
The diviners by stones were telling Susu Sumanguru
    Baamagana,
'A woman is about to give birth
Either this month or next,
And it is a son that she will bear;

620 That is the child who will destroy your reign.'
Sunjata's mother went to the wash-place
And dug a deep hole
Into which she put the infant Sunjata;
Then she put a steamer on top of him.
When dawn broke

She would go and suckle him,
Then replace the steamer on top of him,
And go into town
In search of work.

630   When she had pounded millet for someone,
She used to bring the hard pieces of millet
And pound them
And put them in a steamer like flour.
Sunjata's sister, Nene Faamaga,
And her spirit king were lovers.
They remained like that for three years.
Then the leader of the Kommas came
To Susu Sumanguru Baamagana;
He found Bala Faasigi Kuyate sitting,

640   And Bala said,
    'Cut and Sirimang,
    It is forging and the left hand,
    Senegalese coucal and swallow,
    Cut iron with iron,
    What makes iron valuable,
    Big kuku tree and big silk-cotton tree,
    Fari and Kaunju.'
After that had taken place,
The leader of the Kommas said,

650   'The three years are now completed;
I am going into retreat,
For forty days.
When I come out,
The work which I must do,
I shall do.'
He went into retreat.
When he came out,
He came and found Susu Sumanguru Baamagana sitting.
Bala Faasigi Kuyate was sitting;

660   He jumped to his feet and shouted praises:
    'Great Jaane, Muslim of Manding,

Great Ture, Muslim of Manding,
Great Siise, Muslim of Manding,
Great Komma, Muslim of Manding,
Great Berete, Muslim of Manding,
Saint of saints.'

The leader of the Kommas said, 'Susu Sumanguru Baamagana,
I have served God
For forty days,

670   And from what I have seen,
One must pray
That you remain king till your death,
But you are powerless to prevent this child from becoming
        king.
God has written that down and it cannot be altered.
You must help me with a live porcupine,
One which has not died,
Which has not been shot, but which has been caught and
        brought here,
And from which a quill has been plucked.
I shall make a divinatory pattern with it,

680   And on the skull
Of a child who has been born but died before it was named
I shall make a charm.'
Bala Faasigi Kuyate sought those things;
The leader of the Kommas told him, 'I did not say a child who
        has been seized and had its throat cut;
I said that a child should be born,
But before it was named,
God should come and take its life.
I shall make a charm upon its skull,
And you must bury it in your house.

690   I shall make two patterns,
And put one of them on a stone;
You must find a white stone
And give it to me, along with a piece of paper.
I shall make these two patterns on them

And I shall take them and throw them into the Niger.
When I have thrown them into the river,
The person associated with the one which sinks will die
Between now and your war.'
Four years passed quietly;
700 They did not get a baby for that purpose.
In the fourth year,
A baby was obtained.
It had died, and they got its skull.
That skull
They took to the leader of the Kommas;
Then they went and caught a live porcupine and brought it to
    him;
He plucked out a quill.
They dug up a white stone,
And they chipped it to the shape of a writing board,
710 And took it to him.
They brought him paper;
He went into retreat.
He told Sumanguru, 'On Monday night
You must get into a canoe,
And go and throw this into the Niger,
And you must make a vow upon it;
You must declare that
The person of whom you are afraid,
The person who is to be born in Manding,
720 And who is to destroy your reign,
That his name is on this stone,
And that your name, Susu Sumanguru Baamagana,
Is on the piece of paper.
You must throw them into the Niger;
If one of them sinks,
Then when you and he join battle,
The person associated with that one will perish.'
Sukulung Kutuma,
And Sukulung Yammaru,

730   *Naareng Makhang Konnate,*
       Cats on the shoulder,
       Simbong and Jata are at Naarena;
       Makhang Sunjata's alleged running away,
       The griots made a fine name of it.
       In Sunjata's day in wondrous Manding
       A griot did not have to carry water,
       To say nothing of farming and fetching firewood.
       Father World has changed, changed.
       They sat till midnight on Monday.

740   *Cut and Sirimang,*
       It is forging and the left hand,
       Senegalese coucal and swallow,
       Cut iron with iron,
       And what makes iron valuable,
       Big kuku tree and big silk-cotton tree,
       Fari and Kaunju.
       He and his griot rose up,
       Bala Faasigi Kuyate,
       And got into a canoe, along with a man to paddle it;

750   They threw the stone and the piece of paper into the river.
       Sir, it is of Jata that I speak, great stock,
       Simbong, it is of Jata that I speak, great stock.
       Prince of the Keita line,
       Sukulung Kutuma,
       And Sukulung Yammaru,
       Naareng Makhang Konnate,
       Cats on the shoulder,
       Simbong and Jata are at Naarena.
       He was the son of Khulubu Konte,

760   *Khulubu Konte was the son of Khulubu Khalaba Konte,*
       Sankarang nine boils,
       And six manyang daa.
       Faa Ganda used to kill his in-law on Monday,
       And by the next Monday Faa Ganda was king.
       Sankarang Daminya Konte,

It was he who begat Sukulung Konte,
It was Sukulung Konte who bore Makhang Sunjata.
At that time Sunjata was sitting in the hole;
He was twelve years old,
770   But he could not crawl,
Much less stand up,
Much less walk.
He was just sitting near the house;
He was sitting in his mother's washing enclosure.
When that happened,
They went on till they reached the middle of the Niger.
Susu Sumanguru Baamagana declared,
'I kept two white chickens in my compound,
The leader of the Siises told me
780   That I should do so as a votive offering.
I kept these two white chickens in my compound,
And the child's namesake killed my namesake.
I kept two white rams in my compound;
The leader of the Jaanes told me
That I should do that as an offering.
The child's namesake killed my namesake.
The leader of the Kommas has prepared
A stone and a piece of paper
And said to throw them into the Niger.
790   When I throw them in,
If one of them goes down into the water,
Then the person associated with it is doomed.'
He threw the stone and piece of paper into the water;
The paper spun round and round and then settled at the
       bottom of the river and the stone floated.
From this event the griots say:
Tuu taro jii,
Nii ke laa bere la jii kang,
Bere jee ni wuya.
That is one of Sunjata's songs;
800   I shall come to that in the course of my narration.

Don't you know, Makhang Sunjata is cold;
He was the son of Sukulung Kutuma
And Sukulung Yammaru.
Naareng Makhang Konnate,
Cats on the shoulder,
Simbong and Jata are at Naarena.
Both he and Faa Koli Kumba-and-
Faa Koli Daaba distinguished themselves in Manding.
He came from Woliwolinki,

810 *Great Tambaki, Magasugu Gandana,*
Kutu Yokhobila,
Sina Yokhobila,
Karata Kobila,
Great Bahala Nangang Musa,
And Fitaga Musa,
Bula Banna Gajola.
The royal drums sounded for his grandfather.
Great Bagadugu and Ginate,
Great Hanjulu and Hamina Yanga.

820 (The last two lines refer to Jinna Musa;
Jinna Musa was the father of Faa Koli Kumba,
And the father of Faa Koli Daaba.
Faa Koli Kumba and Faa Koli Daaba
Left Manding with a spear and a bow;
He was Sunjata's military commander.)
Sumanguru returned,
He came home,
And summoned the leader of the Kommas.
The latter said to Sumanguru,

830 'What you have to enjoy,
You must enjoy before this boy grows up.'
Sunjata was then thirteen years old.
Sumanguru summoned the leader of the Tures,
And he told him, 'I want
You to help me.
This child who wishes to destroy my reign –

I no longer aspire to destroy his kingship,
But you must pray for me
That before I die
840 No one will remove me from the kingship,
But that I may remain king.'
The leader of the Serahuli, Mansa Farang Tunkara,
Was at that time king in his own territory.
Sunjata was then fourteen years old.
That year Manding had to hold a circumcision ceremony,
But at that time Sunjata
Could not crawl,
Much less stand up,
Much less walk.
The baobab tree which was in the middle of the town of
850 Manding
Had produced a single fruit, high up;
All Manding was guarding that baobab tree –
The Komma section provided a hundred men,
The Jaane section provided a hundred men,
The Ture section provided a hundred men,
The Siise section provided a hundred men,
The Berete section provided a hundred men,
Susu Sumanguru Baamagana's section provided a hundred
men;
They placed dry wood all round that baobab tree,
860 And they guarded it
Night and day, all the time,
So that when the baobab fruit fell no one else might swallow
the seed
But that Susu Sumanguru Baamagana might get it.
They appointed a day for the circumcision ceremony,
And they proclaimed that on the fourteenth day of the next
month
They would hold a circumcision ceremony in Manding.
Every section was to enter a hundred boys;
Every boy who was to go into the bush

Would mount a horse,
870   With a gun in his hand
And wearing a sword.
When the smith had circumcised you,
You fired your gun and mounted your horse.
Sunjata called his mother,
And his sister Nene Faamaga,
And he said, 'Mother,'
And she replied, 'Yes.'
He said to her, 'My brothers will never go to circumcision
And leave me here.'
880   His mother wept,
And she said to him, 'Sunjata,
I give thanks to God this day.
Forty sons have I borne,
And all have died in the Prophet's war at Haibara.
You have no father,
You have no uncle,
You have no older brother,
You have no step-mother,
You have no aunt,
890   You have no slave,
I have no possessions,
Except this one sister of yours,
Nene Faamaga.'
. . . .
Sunjata's mother wept;
He said to her, 'Mother, my brothers will never go to
      circumcision
910   And leave me here.'
Sunjata's mother, Sukulung Konte, took the road;
She went and stood by the leader of the smiths, Susu
      Sumanguru Baamagana,
And she addressed him, 'Susu Sumanguru Baamagana,
I have come to you.'
He said, 'Why?'

She answered, 'My child who is unable to walk
Says that when the circumcision ceremony is held he too will
   go to circumcision';
She added, 'I have no slave,
And he has no uncle.'
920 When she had spoken these words
To Susu Sumanguru Baamagana,
He said to her,
'And what do you say that I should do?'
She answered, 'I say that you should help me
So that my son may rise up and walk.'
Sumanguru said, 'All right.'
The leader of the griots, Bala Faasigi Kuyate, stood up,
And he said, *'Cut and Sirimang,*
It is forging and the left hand,
930 *Senegalese coucal and swallow,*
Cut iron with iron,
What makes iron valuable,
Big kuku *tree and big silk-cotton tree,*
Fari and Kaunju.'
He continued, 'Defender of orphans,
Forge iron and give it to him so that he may rise up.'
As you know, when someone's leg is broken,
The smiths fashion a staff which they give to him,
And he puts it under his arm –
940 Two such staffs.
Susu Sumanguru Baamagana
Sounded the drums and the young smiths assembled;
He ordered them to quarry ore and fashion it.
They quarried iron ore and smelted it,
And they fashioned it into a very long rod.
They cut it in two
And they bent it.
Three full-grown men took each rod and brought it.
They found Sunjata sitting in his mother's doorway –
950 *Sukulung Kutuma,*

And Sukulung Yammaru,
Naareng Makhang Konnate,
Cats on the shoulder,
Simbong and Jata are at Naarena,
Bone-breaking Lion,
Tie Manding Simbara and untie Simbara.
They laid the rods down beside him, and he laughed,
And said, 'Mother,
These rods cannot accomplish my rising up.

960   When the day comes for me to rise up,'
He said, 'That day I shall rise up.
But I must tell you this,
My brothers will not go to circumcision and leave me here.'
When he put his weight on the rods,
He pressed his hands on the ground, and the rods buckled;
He grabbed them, he picked them up and flung them away
        from where he was sitting.
The people were afraid, and they went and told Susu
        Sumanguru Baamagana.
That day he summoned diviners by stones,
He summoned diviners by cowries,

970   He summoned diviners by sand,
He summoned Muslim diviners,
And they looked into matters concerning Sunjata.
They told Sumanguru, 'The child who will destroy your
        kingship – this is he.'
Sumanguru said, 'This one who is sitting like that, unable to
        move?'
They said, 'Yes.'
Sumanguru said, 'In that case I shall employ a stratagem against
        him before he gets up and stands on his feet.'
He went to the owners of fetishes,
And to the owners of medicine powders,
And to the *korte* men,
And there was much coming and going between him and

980   them.

They tried everything against Sunjata;
He was sitting, unable to move,
Till the day when they had to hold the circumcision
    ceremony.
The uncircumcised boys went into the bush to pick baobab
    leaves
And they dried them for their mothers,
Who pounded those baobab leaves and winnowed them and
    set down the powder.
The Lion was sitting at his mother's doorway;
He did not budge
Until the day before the boys were to go into circumcision,
The day when women were putting into steamers the
990   couscous
Which the circumcision candidates would eat before going
    into the bush;
Sunjata's mother got up.
When she went into town,
Whenever she begged anyone for baobab leaf to put on
    Sunjata's couscous,
That person would say to her, 'You don't know what you are
    saying.
My child who is in good health –
The baobab leaf which he went and picked for me
He brought here
And dried,
1000 And I pounded it,
And I shall put it on his couscous.
I shall not put any of my child's baobab leaf on your child's
    couscous,
That child of yours who is deformed and shapeless
And a cripple,
Who has no mother,
No father,
No uncle,
No brother,

No slave,

1010   No horse –

How is he going to go to circumcision?

Don't make fun of me.'

His mother came home in tears in the evening.

Sunjata said to her, 'Mother, what are you crying about?'

She said to him, 'I went to look for baobab leaf in town;

I intended to put it on the food you would eat the evening
    before you went to circumcision.

Whoever I asked for baobab leaf

Refused me

And said that my son who is deformed and shapeless –

1020   Did I think that they would take some of their baobab leaf

And give to me to put on his food?'

Sunjata laughed,

And he said to his mother, 'Today you will have no more
    worries about baobab leaf.'

Sukulung Kutuma,

And Sukulung Yammaru,

Naareng Makhang Konnate,

Cats on the shoulder,

Simbong and Jata are at Naarena,

Bone breaking Lion,

1030   *Tie Simbara and untie Simbara,*

He came from Khulubu Konte

And Khulubu Khalaba Konte,

Sankarang's six boils

And six manyang daa.

Faa Ganda killed his in-law on Monday,

The following Monday, Faa Ganda was king.

He came from Sankarang Daminya Konte.

Sunjata arose in this fashion:

He grasped the eaves of his mother's house,

1040   He arose and stood up,

He laid his hands upon the middle of the roof, high up;

He called upon God three times,
And he stretched out his hand.
The baobab tree which stood in the middle of the town of
    Manding,
And which slaves were guarding,
And armed men were guarding –
Sunjata seized that baobab tree and twisted it,
And laid it at his mother's doorway.
He split open the baobab fruit and swallowed it.
1050 To his mother he said, 'Here is some baobab leaf!'
The fourteen drums of Manding all sounded.
Susu Sumanguru Baamagana and his griots all rose to their feet,
Along with his attendants,
And they came and found Sunjata standing with his hand
    resting upon the roof of the house.
His mother was weeping,
His sister was weeping;
He said to his mother, 'Pick some baobab leaf!'
Susu Sumanguru Baamagana demanded, 'Who felled this
    baobab tree?'
Sunjata answered, 'I, Sunjata.'
1060 Sumanguru asked, 'Why did you fell the baobab tree?'
Sunjata replied, 'My mother went to look for baobab leaf in
    the town,
To put on the food I was to eat before going into
    circumcision,
But she got no baobab leaf.
She was told to order me to go and pick baobab leaf;
That is why I felled this baobab tree.'
Sumanguru demanded, 'What about the baobab fruit?'
Sunjata replied, 'I have swallowed it.'
Sumanguru asked, 'Why did you swallow the fruit of this
    baobab tree?'
Sunjata answered, 'Now you have come to the point,
1070 Now you have come to it,'
(In the eastern dialect, 'I bara naa kuma di').

Sunjata continued, 'I don't want it,
I don't want anything in Manding,
Except a son,
An older sister,
A wife,
An attendant,
A griot,
And a smith.'

1080 Susu Sumanguru Baamagana said, 'What did you say?'
Sunjata answered, 'That is what I said.'
Sumanguru said, 'Ni wadi,'
That is, 'We are against each other.'
Susu Sumanguru Baamagana turned his back on Sunjata.
His griot proclaimed: *'Cut and Sirimang,*
It is forging and the left hand,
Senegalese coucal and swallow,
Cut iron with iron,
What makes iron valuable,
1090 *Big kuku tree and big silk-cotton tree,*
Fari and Kaunju.'
He said, *'The smith who brings out the* koma *masquerader is in the*
     forefront of the smiths,
Fataga Magaso is in the forefront of the smiths,
A smith of pure blood is in the forefront of the smiths.'
Sumanguru sounded the drum which summoned the people to
     assembly,
He called together all the smiths
Who were to perform the circumcision,
And he addressed them: 'Tomorrow when the circumcision
     candidates go into the bush,
The boy who is called Sunjata –
You must cut off his genitals completely and remove them so
1100   that he dies.'
There was one elderly man there who said, 'Ah, that is not at
     all a simple matter,
Because if we are to do that,

With four hundred and one candidates
One does not know which is Sunjata;
The smiths who are coming
Will not be able to distinguish Sunjata from the others;
What if they were to do that to someone else's child?
We would murder each other in the bush.'
'That is true,' the others said;

1110 'In that case let us load a gun with powder
And put one metal bullet in it
And give it to someone,
Because when they have circumcised a candidate he fires a
    gun;
When Sunjata fires his gun,
The person with the gun with the bullet in it will shoot him
    and he will die.'
One man declared, 'That also is not feasible,
Because if we give this gun to someone and he fires it,
What happens if the bullet goes right through Sunjata and
    comes out and then enters the body of someone else's child?
Or what if the bullet misses Sunjata and goes and kills someone
    else?

1120 There would certainly be fighting then.'
They said, 'Let's leave him.'
Then Susu Sumanguru Baamagana said,
'Let's leave him; let him go into the bush;
Before he comes out of the circumcision area
I shall think of something that will enable me to kill him.'
Sukulung Kutuma,
And Sukulung Yammaru,
Naareng Makhang Konnate
Don't you know that death spares no one at all,

1130 *Don't you realize that Makhang Sunjata is cold;*
Their day is past.
Sunjata is descended from whom and whom?
He is descended from Sukulung Kutuma
And Sukulung Yammaru.

Naareng Makhang Konnate,
Cats on the shoulder,
Simbong and Jata are at Naarena.
His mother's side is
Dugu and Bala,
1140 *Faabaga and Taulajo,*
Supreme horseman whom none surpasses,
Wuruwarang Kaba,
Dala Kumbukamba,
And Dala Jiibaa Minna,
Kasawura Konte.
Sukulung Konte was descended from Sukulung Kuma,
The latter was descended from Khulubu Konte
Khulubu Konte was the father of Khulubu Khalaba Konte,
Khulubu Khalaba Konte was the father of Sankarang Daminya
  Konte,
Sankarang Daminya Konte was the father of Faabaga and
1150 *Taulajo,*
Faabaga and Taulajo was the father of Sankarang Madiba Konte,
Sankarang Madiba Konte was the father of Sukulung Kutuma
  Konte,
And she it was who bore Sunjata.

Sunjata and the other boys went to the circumcision area.
While they were there,
Susu Sumanguru Baamagana summoned the head of the Ture
    family,
And said to him, 'I set the head of the Jaane family to work
To find a countermeasure to this child, but we did not find
    one.
He prescribed two white rams for me as a votive offering;
1160 The child's namesake killed my namesake.
I set the head of the Siise family to work
To find a countermeasure to this child, but we did not find
    one.
He prescribed two white chickens for me as an offering;
The child's namesake killed my namesake.

I set the head of the Komma family to work
Against this child.
He prepared stone and paper,
And I took them to the Niger;
The one with my name attached to it sank,
The one with the child's name attached to it came to the
1170   surface.
Head of the Ture family and head of the Berete family,' he
     said,
'I have given you the task of dealing with this child.
He is in the circumcision area.
He is in the bush,
And before he leaves it,
You must think of some means of destroying him.'
In Mandinka, that means
He gave the task of dealing with the child to these two men,
Great Ture, Muslim of Manding, and great Berete, Muslim of
     Manding,
1180 And they had to work against Sunjata
Before he left the circumcision area.
The head of the Tures
And the head of the Beretes
Set to work
And prepared *naso*.
When they wrote on the writing-board,
For one month and fourteen days
They wrote on the board – the *bisimalato* pattern.
They prepared names,
1190 They made calculations from God's names
And they put them in the *naso*,
And they added special ingredients,
And then they took it to Susu Sumanguru Baamagana.
They said to him, 'If you put this *naso* in your wash-place,
And stop up the mouth of the container for forty days,
When the forty days are up,
If you wash yourself with the *naso*,

And if the child does not see you
And nothing has spoilt the *naso*,
1200   You will die in office,
But this child will never be king here in Manding.
When you have washed yourself with it at midnight,
That night you must come out, wet with that *naso*,
And walk round all four gates of Manding,
And you must walk round all four corners of Manding
That night before dawn breaks.
Then this child,' they said,
'Will never be king.'
During this time,
1210   Sunjata's sister, Nene Faamaga,
Was talking with her spirit king, Yura,
One Friday night.
Manga Yura said to her,
'They have contrived a stratagem against your brother,
And if it succeeds,
Then his prospects of becoming king are destroyed.'
'What sort of a stratagem is it?' she asked.
He told her, 'They are making *naso*,
And they are putting special ingredients in it.
If Susu Sumanguru Baamagana succeeds in washing with that
1220   *naso*,
If he goes round the four gates of Manding,
If he walks through the town of Manding,
Then Sunjata's prospects of becoming king are destroyed.'
She said to him, 'Won't you help us then?
For the sake of love, my life is in your hands,
And you must support us;
We have no mother,
We have no father,
We are orphans,
1230   We have no uncle.'
He replied, 'All right,
On the eve of the appointed day

I shall remove you and Sunjata both from the circumcision
    area
And I shall take you to the wash-place;
When Sumanguru is about to wash himself with the *naso*,
I shall give your father's sword to Sunjata
And he can fall upon Susu Sumanguru Baamagana
And prevent him from washing with the *naso*.
They will fight there in the wash-place.

1240 If that *naso* is spilt,' he said,
'Susu Sumanguru Baamagana's reign will be destroyed,
And nothing will stop Sunjata from becoming king.'
She said, 'Praise be to God.'
He went on, 'Today they have put the *naso* in the wash-place;
Thirty-nine days from today,
On the eve of the fortieth day,
I shall come for you and I shall take you to the circumcision
    area,
And I shall take Sunjata out of there,
And I shall take him to the wash-place.

1250 Whatever is needed, I shall give to Sunjata there.'
Sir, it is of Lion that I speak, great stock,
Simbong, it is of Lion that I speak, the man of great stock is a man of
    power.
Praise be to God, Master of the worlds.
. . . .

They sat quietly for thirty-nine days;
On the eve of the fortieth day
Kaata Yura

1270 Arrived at Sunjata's sister's house.
It had just got dark when the spirit king arrived,
Along with his griot and his xylophone.
It was on that occasion that the xylophone made its first
    appearance.
When people had finished their evening meal
And were starting to go to bed,
Sunjata's sister, Nene Faamaga,

And her spirit king,
Manga Yura –
He placed Nene Faamaga upon his back
1280   And flew into the air with her.
They went to the circumcision area
And he covered up the eyes of the man in charge of the
    circumcision area,
And all those in the circumcision area
He put to sleep.
He laid Sunjata upon Nene Faamaga's back
And they flew away to the stronghold.
He deposited Sunjata inside Susu Sumanguru Baamagana's
    wash-place
And he left him standing there.
He went for Sunjata's father's long sword,
1290   And came and put it in Sunjata's hand.
When it was midnight,
They were standing in the wash-place,
And Susu Sumanguru Baamagana and his griot and his two
    attendants came out of the house and into the wash-place.
Sumanguru undressed, laid down his amulets,
Sat on a white stone,
Put his hand on top of the jar containing ablution water,
And said, 'The head of the Siise family prescribed
Two white chickens as a votive offering.
I gave two white chickens as an offering.
1300   The boy's namesake got the better of my namesake.
The head of the Komma family prescribed
Two white rams as an offering.
I gave two white rams as an offering.
The boy's namesake got the better of my namesake.
The head of the Jaane family prepared
Stone and paper.
I put them in the Niger.
The one bearing my name sank, and the one bearing the boy's
    name came to the surface.

The head of the Tures and the head of the Beretes
1310   Prepared this *naso*,
And they declared that if I wash with it,
Within four days,
If the boy does not see me,
If I walk round the four gates of Manding,
Then when I complete it,
I shall be master of Manding
Till I die,
And Sunjata will never be in control of Manding.'
He put his hand into the *naso*,
1320   And was about to sprinkle it on himself,
When Sunjata swiftly drew his sword
And demanded of him, 'What did you say?'
Sumanguru replied, 'I didn't say anything!'
Sunjata said, 'Yes,
What did you say?'
Sumanguru said, 'I did not speak.'
(In Mandinka that is 'I did not speak'.)
Sunjata demanded, 'What did you say?'
Sumanguru replied, 'I didn't say anything!'
1330   Sunjata ordered, 'Pour it away!', and he poured it away.
Sunjata ordered, 'Dig a hole!', and he dug a hole.
Sunjata ordered, 'Put your amulets in it!', and he put them in
    it.
Sunjata ordered, 'Fill it in!', and he filled it in.
Sunjata ordered, 'Urinate on it!', and he urinated on it.
Sunjata said to Sumanguru's griot, 'Sing this man's praises,
    please.'
The griot said, *'Cut and Sirimang,*
It is forging and the left hand,
Senegalese coucal and swallow,
Cut iron with iron,
1340   *What makes iron valuable,*
Big kuku tree and big silk-cotton tree.'
Sunjata shouted, 'Stop there!'

Then he said, 'Call him by the name Kante – *n kang te.*'
He ordered the griot, 'Now sing my praises, please.'
And the griot said, *'Dugu and Bala,*
Faabaga and Taulajo,
Wuruwarang Kaba,
Dala Kumbukamba,
And Dala Jiibaa Minna,
1350 *Kasawura Konte,*
Sukulung Kutuma
And Sukulung Yammaru,
Naareng Makhang Konnate,
Cats on the shoulder,
Simbong and Jata are at Naarena,
Bone-breaking Lion,
Tie Manding Simbara
And untie Simbara.'
It was that day that he said:
1360 *Thatching grass, thatching grass, thatching grass,*
Other things go underneath thatching grass,
Thatching grass does not go underneath anything.
The spirit picked up Sunjata and his sister
And took them to the circumcision area.
They were there till the day when the newly circumcised boys
    were leaving the circumcision area;
It was on that day that Sunjata was given his own tune.
His mother,
Sukulung Konte, said
That the child whom she had borne
1370 Had been carried in her womb for twelve years;
Some people had said that it was a disease,
Others had said that it was an illness causing swelling of the
    abdomen,
Others had said that it was worms,
Others had said that it was all sorts of things.
At length she had given birth to that child,
And for fourteen years the child was a cripple;

He just sat, and did not walk.

Was it that child who was coming thus in the attire of a newly
    circumcised boy?

Sunjata has come, Sumanguru,

1380   *Sunjata has come, Sumanguru.*

Sumanguru was the king who was in control of Manding at
    that time.

Sunjata has come, Sumanguru.

Ah, Sunjata is a cripple,

Sunjata has come, Sumanguru.

Sunjata said:

Thatching grass, thatching grass, thatching grass,

Other things go underneath thatching grass,

Thatching grass does not go underneath anything.

Thatching grass, thatching grass, thatching grass,

1390   *Others run away from Sunjata,*

Sunjata does not run away from anyone.

A soap-taking dog,

A dog which does not leave soap alone,

It will not leave a bone alone,

Sunjata ding kasi kang, Sumanguru.

Death is better than disgrace, Sumanguru.

Kankinya,

Kankinya, griot, Kankinya,

Kankinya, there is a gate at Kankinya,

1400   *War at Kankinya.*

Kankinya was Susu Sumanguru's stronghold.

When Sunjata had entered Manding,

That night Susu Sumanguru Baamagana prepared for war;

He attacked Sunjata's mother's compound

And burned it to the ground, and he captured Sunjata.

But Sunjata escaped

And went to Mansa Farang Tunkara.

He lived there,

And at night he would sally forth and come into Manding;

He would take an army and destroy the whole of one area of
1410   Manding,
And then retire.
Susu Sumanguru would pursue him,
But when they reached Mansa Farang Tunkara's territory,
Sumanguru would turn back.
Sunjata's sister
Was married to a spirit,
Whose name, as you are aware, was Manga Yura.
One day Manga Yura said to his wife,
'If you want to overcome Sumanguru,
1420   You won't do it by fighting.
A spear and an arrow, that is what will kill him.'
Spear and arrow in Mandinka,
If you say spear and arrow,
That is bow and spear.
That spear was in the possession of the head of the Sooras.
Jinna Musa came to Sunjata;
He found him at Mansa Farang Tunkara's place.
He gave him a charm,
And told Sunjata that he was to go on pilgrimage to Mecca
1430   And he would pray for him till he secured Manding.
Jinna Musa went on pilgrimage to Mecca.
When he returned,
He brought a spear,
The spear Tuluku Muluku, *One place where it enters, nine places
      where blood comes forth.*
They call him Kiliya Musa,
Nooya Musa,
Bula Wuruwuru,
And Bala Wanjaga,
Futu Yokhobila,
1440   *Sina Yokhobila,*
Bimba Yokhobila,
Baha la nankang Musa,
And Fitaga Musa.

He it was who brought the spear, the bow and the arrow.
He it was who begat Faa Koli Kumba
And Faa Koli Daaba.
These two people joined Makhang Sunjata,
And they fought alongside him.
They used to come to Manding with him;
1450 They lived at Mansa Farang Tunkara's place.
Sunjata's sister, Nene Faamaga, came and said to him,
'I want you to come to my spirit king
So that he can help you.'
Indeed, it is of Lion that I speak, great stock,
Simbong, it is of Lion that I speak, great stock.
Great God,
Sukulung Kutuma
And Sukulung Yammaru here,
Naareng Makhang Konnate,
1460 *Cats on the shoulder,*
Simbong and Jata are at Naarena.
In Sunjata's day a griot did not have to fetch water,
To say nothing of farming and gathering firewood.
Father World has changed, changed.
One day when Sunjata had to come to the hill called Yura,
The spirit king came with his griot and xylophone.
At that time Bala Faasigi Kuyate
Belonged to Susu Sumanguru Baamagana in Manding.
Sunjata and Faa Koli Kumba and Faa Koli Daaba were sitting
1470 In his sister's house.
The spirit king, Manga Yura, arrived
With the xylophone, which they played like this –
(This is Manga Yura's tune).
When Sunjata heard the xylophone
He asked his sister,
'What sort of instrument is making that noise?'
She replied, 'It is my husband who is coming with it,
He and his griot, but I don't know what it is.'
Sunjata declared, 'In that case I will kill your husband today

1480　And take this instrument.'
　　　She asked, 'Are you going to kill him?'
　　　He answered, 'Yes.'
　　　She said, 'This is the person who helped you.'
　　　Sunjata said, 'I will kill him today.'
　　　They went under the bed.
　　　When the spirit king arrived, he stood in the doorway,
　　　And he said to his wife,
　　　'Nene Faamaga,' and she replied.
　　　He went on, 'I shall not sleep in this house today
1490　Unless I dismantle the bed.'
　　　She said, 'It was my brother who erected this bed,
　　　It is not going to be dismantled.'
　　　He said, 'Ah, Nene Faamaga,
　　　This is the eve of Friday;
　　　I shall not sleep on the bed,
　　　Only on the floor.
　　　I shall pull up the forked sticks supporting the bed,
　　　And lie on the floor.
　　　Nene Faamaga,' he added,
　　　'Nothing happens under the plait which the louse does not
1500　　know about.
　　　Your brother who is lying under the bed –
　　　Tell him to come out.'
　　　Sunjata came out.
　　　The long-barrelled gun which he had
　　　He let fly at the spirit king.
　　　It split apart right to the butt.
　　　The spirit king lay on the bed laughing.
　　　At that time Bala Faasigi Kuyate was a member of Susu
　　　　Sumanguru Baamagana's household.
　　　Faa Koli Kumba came out from under the bed and drew an
　　　　arrow
1510　And fired it at the spirit king;
　　　The arrow shattered completely.

Faa Koli Daaba came out from under the bed with a round
   iron rod,
And he lifted it up and held his two hands up like this.
The spirit king said to Nene Faamaga,
'You have shamed me.
So it is,
The spirits are saying that I have married just an insignificant
   human,
That I have pursued nothing but an insignificant human.
If you want the xylophone,
1520   Tell me, and I will give it to your brother,
But I think that my life does not count for as much with you
   as the xylophone does.'
It was that day that Sunjata got the xylophone;
He went away with the xylophone;
He went to Mansa Farang Tunkara's place with it,
And he hung up the xylophone.
No one played it except Sunjata himself.
Susu Sumanguru Baamagana devised a plan
And gave orders that Sunjata be summoned;
When he came to Manding,
1530   They must say to him that he is a prince,
That they are smiths and that they must return the land to him;
Since his brothers were in Manding,
He ought not to flee from his father's home
And go and live in the land of the Tunkaras.
They sent Bala Faasigi Kuyate to deliver the summons;
Bala Faasigi Kuyate's name originated from that.
When Bala Faasigi Kuyate arrived,
He explained his mission to Mansa Farang Tunkara
In these words: 'The people of Manding have sent me
1540   With orders to come for Sunjata;
He must go to Manding,
He must go and be king,
Because he is a son of the royal line.
He ought not to run away

And come and live here.'
Sunjata rushed up to him
And declared, 'You have spoken the truth.'
He took down the xylophone,
And Bala Faasigi Kuyate asked him, 'What is this?'
1550   Sunjata answered, 'I myself got this from a relative of mine.'
He took down the xylophone and gave it to him.
As soon as Bala Faasigi had played the xylophone,
Sunjata grabbed his two Achilles tendons and cut them,
And he told Bala Faasigi, 'You will not go back again.
You must stay here and play the xylophone for me;
You must be my griot.'
That is why he is called Bala Faasigi;
They cut his tendons and they called him Bala Faasigi –
'You will settle here.'
1560   His name was Musa,
But they called him Bala Faasigi Kuyate;
When they had cut these two tendons,
They told him, 'Settle here!'
That is why they gave him the xylophone.
Sunjata's sister left home
And went to Mansa Farang Tunkara
And told him, 'I have come to my brother
So that he may let me go
And marry Susu Sumanguru Baamagana.
1570   Sumanguru will certainly never know me as a wife,
Since he is a smith.'
After Sunjata's sister
Had said that she was going to marry Susu Sumanguru
    Baamagana,
She came and found Susu Sumanguru and his griots sitting.
His griots shouted his praises,
'*Cut and Sirimang,*
It is forging and the left hand,
Senegalese coucal and swallow,
Cut iron with iron,

1580   *What makes iron valuable,*
   Big kuku *tree and big silk-cotton tree.'*
To Sunjata's sister they said, 'Greetings!',
And she returned the greeting.
Bala Faasigi Kuyate
Said to her,
'Nene Faamaga, what have you come here for?'
She told him, 'I have come to marry Susu Sumanguru
   Baamagana.'
Susu Sumanguru Baamagana raised himself up into a sitting
   position
And asked her, 'What did you say?'
She replied, 'I have come to marry Susu Sumanguru
1590   Baamagana.'
He asked her, 'What for? –
Your brother and I, Susu Sumanguru Baamagana, are enemies;
It is now seven years
That we have been waging war by every available means.
Your brother wishes to make himself master of Manding;
How comes it that you could marry Susu Sumanguru
   Baamagana?'
She replied, 'I have talked with Sunjata,
But he took no heed of what I said,
Because he is my younger brother,
1600   Whom I have carried upon my back.
Since he refuses to listen to me,
I wash my hands of him,
And I will marry Susu Sumanguru Baamagana,
And my brother will see me in his keeping,
And there is nothing that he will be able to do about it.'
They were married that very day.
When Susu Sumanguru Baamagana and Sunjata's sister went to
   bed at night,
He put his hand on her,
But she removed his hand;
1610   He asked her, 'What is the matter?'

And she answered, 'I am the daughter of a king,
You too are a king;
You will know me as a wife,
But you have not told me about yourself.'
'About myself?' he said.
She said to him, 'You have not told me
What it is that can kill you –
Why then should I marry you?
Why should you know me as a wife?
1620   For what good reason?
Besides, you are a smith, I am a princess.
In fact, I am marrying you because of some magical power of
        yours;
You must tell me what that magical power is,
That power which can kill you.'
He raised his hand and laid it upon her again,
And she said to him, 'Only if you tell me
About yourself!'
He was about to speak
When his mother, who was in the house,
1630   Cleared her throat
And said to him, 'Susu Sumanguru Baamagana,
My child, don't ruin yourself.
Is a one-night woman
Going to destroy your whole world?
You and this woman's brother are at war,
Night and day.
You attack each other with *korte*,
You assail each other through diviners,
And now you say that that man's sister is to marry you,
1640   When she lies down at your back,
You will reveal all about yourself in that one night.'
He said to Nene Faamaga, 'Wait;
When my mother is asleep, I will tell you what you want to
        know.'
She replied, 'All right, when your mother has fallen asleep,

And you have told me,
Then will you know me as a wife,
But if you do not tell me how you can be killed,
You will not know me as a wife.'
When his mother had fallen asleep,
1650 He laid his hand upon Nene Faamaga.
She said to him,
'You shall not know me as a wife
Unless you tell me what will kill you.'
He replied, 'A spear will not kill me,
An arrow will not kill me,
A gun will not kill me,
Korte will not kill me,
Witchcraft will not kill me;
There is only one thing,' he said, 'which will kill me:
1660 A one-year-old cock which crows,
Provided it is a white fowl.'
He said, 'You will catch it and kill it,
And you must remove its spur,
And you must put pure gold dust and pure silver dust inside it,
And you must put it in a gun.
If you shoot me with that,
I shall die.'
She said to him, 'I shall be menstruating till tomorrow,'
She lay down and they fell asleep.
1670 The cocks crowed;
Nene Faamaga leapt over the town wall and off she went.
She found Sunjata at Bala Faasigi Kuyate's house;
She and Bala Faasigi Kuyate arose
And went to Mansa Farang Tunkara's place.
She said, 'Sunjata,
My younger brother,
You can have a little mother,
You can have a little father,
But you cannot have a little elder sister.
1680 I am your older sister, my brother.

As to a means of killing Susu Sumanguru Baamagana,
There is only one thing that will do that:
A one-year-old cock which crows
Must be seized and killed.
Into that cock's spur you must put silver dust and gold dust.
You must load a gun with powder and put the spur in the
    gun.
That cock's spur,' she said,
'Is what will kill Susu Sumanguru Baamagana.'
Sunjata said, 'All right.'
1690   He summoned Dala Kumbukamba.
At that time the soldiers who were under Sunjata's command:
Jinna Musa's sons,
Faa Koli Kumba
And Faa Koli Daaba,
And Kiliya Musa
And Nooya Musa,
Together with Bala Faasigi Kuyate.
They got ready and they came against Manding.
Sunjata was advised, 'You will not be able to crush Manding
1700   Unless you give a live crocodile as a votive offering,
And take it into the town of Manding;
When it has walked about within the town of Manding,
You will then be able to crush Manding
And to kill Susu Sumanguru Baamagana.'
Sunjata was perplexed.
So he went to the head of the Bozos
And asked him to help him to obtain a live crocodile.
He caught a live crocodile and brought it.
Sunjata said, 'Who will take this live crocodile into Manding
    for me?'
1710   Faa Koli Kumba and Faa Koli Daaba said to him,
'We will take the live crocodile to Manding.'
At that time people used to make clothing from cloth made up
    of strips sewn together;
When weavers had made a cloth –

That cloth made up of strips sewn together – they used to go
    and sell it.
Faa Koli Kumba bought a cloth,
A very big one,
And he wrapped up the crocodile
And put it at his side;
He wrapped up that cloth,
1720 Tied it and took it to Manding.
When he reached the public meeting place in Manding,
The women saw him and rushed up to him saying, 'Here is the
    cloth pedlar!'
He said to them, 'It is already dark;
I shall not sell these cloths till tomorrow.
I am going to sleep here.'
They went and lodged him in a house.
Woliwolinki,
Tambaki great man and Magasugu Ngandana,
Great Bula is cold.
1730 That refers to the head of the Sooras,
Kiliya Musa and Nooya Musa,
Bula Wuruwuru and Bula Wanjaga,
Kutu Yokhobila and Sina Yokhobila,
And Bumbang Yokhobila.
That is Faa Koli Kumba
And Faa Koli Daaba
They fought in Manding with spear and arrow for Sunjata.
They went and lodged him.
After he had gone to bed, when night had fallen and midnight
    come,
1740 He saddled his horse;
He took the cloth and tied it on his horse,
He shut the door and left the live crocodile inside the house.
The diviners by stones and the diviners by cowries had told
Susu Sumanguru Baamagana,
'No one can kill you here
Unless he gives a live crocodile as an offering,

And it walks about inside the town of Manding.
The man who would catch a live crocodile and bring it into
   Manding
Has never been seen by us,
1750 Because we would kill anyone who entered here.'
Sunjata left there and went to Mansa Farang Tunkara's place,
Where he met a man who owned 'black medicine',
Who said to him, 'Koro ming kankang, dung koro ning baajii,
   foroko fila ning falang.'
He said, 'I will prepare a black cat's skin
And make *korte* out of it;
That black cat's skin
Must you take and go to Manding
And give to someone who will drop it down the well in
   Manding.'
Dawn broke; the women jostled each other
1760 As they brought a huge breakfast
For Faa Koli Kumba and Faa Koli Daaba in his house.
When they opened the door the live crocodile
Came waddling out of the house.
There was a commotion, and the drums were sounded;
Men said, 'Susu Sumanguru Baamagana,
The stranger who slept here last night
Brought a crocodile into this town as a votive offering.'
They caught the crocodile
And tied it up;
1770 Faa Koli Kumba and Faa Koli Daaba
Came with his spear that day to Manding;
He said to Sunjata, 'The black cat's skin –
They killed a black cat and made it into a leather bag and put
   naso in it.
If someone takes that *naso*
And drops it down the well of Manding,
That Manding well which is in the middle of the town,
The day that he drops it down there,
And that the people of Manding drink water from that well,

That day will you crush Manding.'
When the drums sounded, all the people of Manding gathered
1780   at the public meeting-place,
By one of their gatehouses;
They were sitting near that well;
They had tied up the live crocodile and laid it down.
Susu Sumanguru Baamagana arose and declared,
'Whoever finds the trader
Who brought this crocodile here into this town
Must seize him and bring him here.'
He would divide Manding into two parts,
And he would give one part to the man who found the trader,
    and he would be in control of it.
1790   Sibi Kamara, head of the Kamaras, arose –
That head of the Kamaras, Sibi Kamara,
Begat Hamana Kamara,
And he begat also Baliya Kamara.
Baliya Kamara begat Foobali Dumbe,
Foobali Dumbe begat Makhang Kuta Kamara,
Makhang Kuta Kamara begat Juhuna Kamara,
Juhuna Kamara begat Tamba Bukari,
Tamba Bukari begat Soona Kamara,
Soona Kamara bore Almami Samori.
1800   Sibi Kamara declared that he would go and fetch the person
Who had brought the crocodile there.
He would seek him out,
With fetish he would seek him out,
With *korte* he would seek him out,
With the help of a diviner by stones he would seek him out.
They were just at that point
When Soora Musa Bankang [Faa Koli],
Kiliya Musa and Nooya Musa,
Bula Wuruwuru and Bula Wanjaga,
1810   Arrived on horseback with the bag made out of a black cat.
He came and found the people sitting at the public
    meeting-place.

He galloped past
And came upon some women beside the well;
He spurred his white stallion,
Which raised its two forelegs
And placed them on the low wall surrounding the well;
He put his hand into his leather bag
And withdrew the black cat's skin,
And declared: 'People of Manding,

1820   I am Soora Musa Bankang,
Kiliya Musa and Nooya Musa, Bula Wuruwuru.
It was Sunjata who sent me,
With orders to throw this black cat's skin as an offering
Down your well.'
He threw it down the well.
There was an uproar and the drum sounded.
They rushed upon him and he spurred his white stallion.
He had a spear that day
And the name of that spear was Tuluku Muluku, *One place
    where it enters, nine places where the blood comes out.*

1830   When you hear people called Soora, their surname is Susokho.
He spurred his horse.
When he spurred his horse with the stirrups,
The horse leapt up with him;
Whenever he struck anyone a single blow with the spear,
If he pierced him in one place,
Blood would come out of nine places altogether in his body.
Finally he went right through the crowd
And out at the other side;
He went and found Sunjata at Bala Faasigi Kuyate's place.

1840   He found Bala Faasigi Kuyate and Sunjata sitting;
He said to them, 'I have washed the black cat.
I have thrown it down the well.
I found the people sitting with a live crocodile at the four gates
    of Manding.'
Bala Faasigi Kuyate arose and shouted,
'Sukulung Kutuma

And Sukulung Yammaru,
Naareng Makhang Konnate,
Cats on the shoulder,
Simbong and Jata are at Naarena,
1850 *Bone-breaking Lion,*
Tie Manding Simbara and untie Manding Simbara,
Dagu and Bala,
Faabaga and Taulajo,
Mighty horseman whom none surpasses,
Wuruwurang Kaba,
Dala Kumbukamba,
And Dala Jiibaa Minna,
Sankarang Madiba Konte,
He it was who was the father of Sukulung Konte
1860 *She it was who bore you, Makhang Sunjata.'*
Sunjata arose,
And went and seized a white cock that day,
And killed it.
When he had killed the white cock,
They plucked it and singed it;
They burned its feet and removed the spurs,
They put silver dust and gold dust inside,
They loaded a gun and put it in the hands of Faa Koli Kumba
    and Faa Koli Daaba.
They came and circled round Manding, the three of them,
1870 Faa Koli Kumba and Faa Koli Daaba and Sunjata;
Seven times they went round Manding, then they stood still,
They and Bala Faasigi Kuyate.
It was that day that Bala Faasigi Kuyate sang:
Ah, Sunjata has come, Sumanguru,
Ah, Sunjata has come, Sumanguru.
The town drum sounded.
Ah, Sunjata has come, Sumanguru,
Ah, Sunjata is here, Sumanguru.
They sounded the town drum and the whole town came forth.
1880 Sunjata, with his horse,

And his long sword,
And his iron rod,
And his double-barrelled gun with the cock's spur in it.
Susu Sumanguru Baamagana came forth,
With his long sword,
And his iron rod,
And his three-pronged spear,
And his double-barrelled gun.
All of Manding came forth;

1890   They stood at the four wondrous gates,
And they sent forth these two men.
Sunjata said to Susu Sumanguru Baamagana, 'Go ahead.'
Susu Sumanguru Baamagana replied, 'No, you go ahead, you
    are the younger.'
Sunjata answered, 'No, go ahead, you are the older.'
Susu Sumanguru Baamagana took his horse back some
    distance, then he declared: 'This is far enough.'
He charged on horseback with his three-pronged spear;
He raised it aloft and struck Sunjata with it;
The three-pronged spear shattered and fell to the ground.
Sumanguru retired;

1900   There was a great shout.
Faa Koli Kumba and Faa Koli Daaba and Bala Faasigi Kuyate,
Only these three were in support of Sunjata,
Whereas the whole of Manding supported Susu Sumanguru
    Baamagana.
After Susu Sumanguru Baamagana had struck Sunjata
He retired and went a long way off on his horse,
Then he returned.
He struck Sunjata with his long sword;
The long sword broke into three pieces and fell to the ground.
He retired again

1910   Then returned with his iron rod.
He raised it aloft and was about to strike Sunjata with the iron
    rod,
But his arm remained aloft, immovable.

He said to Sunjata, 'Go ahead.'
Sunjata came and struck Sumanguru with his three-pronged
    spear;
The three-pronged spear was shattered.
He retired, then came with a long sword;
The long sword too was shattered and fell to the ground.
When he set his hand to his gun
And raised it and was about to aim at him,
1920 It was then that Susu Sumanguru Baamagana turned tail
And was about to run away.
Sunjata declared:
Sunjata has come, Sumanguru,
Ah, Sunjata is here, Sumanguru.
He went on:
Thatching grass, thatching grass, thatching grass,
Other things go underneath thatching grass,
Thatching grass does not go underneath anything;
Thatching grass, thatching grass, thatching grass,
1930 *Others run away from Sunjata,*
Sunjata does not run from anyone.
A soap-taking dog,
A dog which does not leave soap alone
Will not leave a bone alone.
Sunjata ding kasi kang, Sumanguru,
Death is better than disgrace, Sumanguru.
He produced the chicken spur at that point
And shot Sumanguru with it;
He fell.
1940 It was that day that Sunjata told Bala Faasigi Kuyate,
'Every smith in Manding
Will bear the name Nkante.
I want you to sing the praises of the smiths so that I can hear.'
He declared:
Cut and Sirimang.
It is forging and the left hand,
Senegalese coucal and swallow,

Cut iron with iron,
What makes iron valuable,
1950 *Big* kuku *tree and big silk-cotton tree,*
Fari and Kaunju.
As the Mandinka say, the eastern people understand the
    language of the griots;
All this is meaningful.
He said, '*Sege and Sirimang,*
That is Sunjata and Susu Sumanguru Baamagana.
That is forging and the left hand –
That is pincers and iron.
Cut iron with iron, what makes iron valuable –
That means that one great man gets the better of another great
    man by magical means.
1960 *Big* kuku *tree and big silk-cotton tree –*
That means that however big a silk-cotton tree may be, it
    stands in an even bigger open space.
Fari and Kaunju –
That is the bellows and the small clay mound through which
    the bellows pipe leads into the fire.'

He turned round and presented his back;
Sunjata was standing.
Bala said, '*Dugu and Bala,*
Faabaga and Taulajo,
Supreme horseman whom none surpasses,
Wuruwarang Kaba,
1970 *Dala Kumbukamba and Dala Jiibaa Minna,*
Kasawura Konte,
Sankarang Madiba Konte,
He it was who was the father of Sukulung Konte,
Sukulung Konte it was who bore you, Makhang Sunjata.'
He went on,
It is war which devasted Manding,
It is war which rebuilt Manding,
Sunjata entered Manding with these griots' songs.

They sang:

1980 *Kankinya,*

Kankinya, there is a gate at Kankinya,

Kankinya, there is a gate at Kankinya,

War at Kankinya.

The fortified position occupied by Susu Sumanguru Baamagana

Was called Kankinya.

When Sunjata entered Manding,

He destroyed the four wondrous gates;

He rebuilt them and made them into four gatehouses,

He made them into four gatehouses;

1990 Four little beds were put inside them.

When dawn broke,

Bala Faasigi Kuyate would come

And play this tune – the *Janjungo* tune.

At first cock-crow

He would come and stand at Sunjata's gate;

He would play the *Janjungo* tune and say:

Great Janjung, it is war which shattered Janjung,

War rebuilt great Janjung.

Janjung was the name of that Manding gatehouse.

2000 He would say to Sunjata,

'*Sukulung Kutuma*

And Sukulung Yammaru here,

Nareng Makhang Konnate,

Cats on the shoulder,

Simbong and Jata are at Naarena.

In Sunjata's day a griot did not have to fetch water,

To say nothing of farming and gathering firewood.

Father World has changed, changed.'

Sunjata would come out of his house

2010 And come and sit on his earthen platform

Near his own doorway.

Bala would go and stand by the head of the Sooras

And he would say to him, '*Soora Musa Bankaalu,*

Kiliya Musa and Nooya Musa,

Bula Wuruwuru and Bula Wanjaga,
Kutu Yokhobila and Sina Yokhobila,
And Karta Yokhobila and Bumba Yokhobila.
It was your grandfather who sounded the royal drum to summon
    assemblies,
Mighty Bagadugu and Ginate,
2020 *Mighty Hanjugu and Hamina Yanga.'*
The head of the Sooras would also come out
And come and sit on his earthen platform.
(At that time wooden platforms for sitting on were not built;)
They used to beat earth into a platform,
Which they called *bilingo*.
Each of the four gates had an earthen platform.
He would go to Faa Koli Kumba and to Faa Koli Daaba,
He would go to Sibi Kamara,
And the latter would also come and sit at his gatehouse.
2030 Bala Faasigi Kuyate would come and sit in their midst.
Sunjata was in control of Manding for seven years.
. . . .

Now, white man, the account of Sunjata's career as far as I
    know it,
2065 As I heard it from my parents,
And my teachers,
Ends here.

Notes

Bamba Suso: Sunjata

5   *Sotuma*: a village about eight miles west of Basse Santa Su in Fulladu East, Upper River Division of the Gambia.

7   The accompaniment which is played on the *kora* throughout this entire performance is *Kura* (see Introduction).

12   *Sanimentereng*: a small uninhabited island lying off the coast near Brufut, Kombo North in the Gambia. It is believed to be the abode of many jinns. A person who wishes to secure the aid of these jinns will go to Sanimentereng, after first having received permission to do so from a certain family in Brufut, on a Thursday evening, and will spend the night there, returning to the mainland on Friday. During the night many terrifying apparitions will manifest themselves, but if the person seeking the aid of the jinns remains in control of himself, the leader of the jinns will appear and grant his wish. Some people who have visited Sanimentereng are said to have been driven out of their minds by their experiences during the night that they spent there, and not many people now venture to go there. Though presumably pre-Islamic, the beliefs associated with Sanimentereng have been to some extent adapted to Islam; the jinns are said to be in human form, tall, handsome and dressed in white robes.

15   *simbingo*: a harp-lute, smaller than the *kora*, with a curved neck and only six strings. This is the instrument which is used today by the hunters' griots, that is those griots who are associated with hunters and who specialize in hunters' songs and in narrations which recount the exploits of great hunters.

27   *Fata Kung Makhang*: many important personages in the Sunjata epic have several different names; Sunjata's father is addressed as Naareng Daniyang Konnate in line 75, see Chart 1.

35   There is general agreement among the griots that Sunjata's mother's name was Sukulung.

50   The fact that Sunjata's mother had a fright only once during her long

pregnancy is significant in view of a belief that if a pregnant woman gets a fright this will affect the child by making it less brave than it otherwise would have been. If the mother does not have a fright during her pregnancy, then her child will be brave. The behaviour of the mother is believed by the Mandinka to affect the fortune of her son; the son of a dutiful wife will prosper, whereas the son of an unsatisfactory wife will never amount to anything.

65–81   The incident recounted here of the two messengers, the second of whom delivers his message first, is a common motif in Africa, found in myths about the origin of death. H. Abrahamsson (1951) regards the myth of the Message that Failed as the commonest African myth, explaining how death came into the world. Abrahamsson gives the most common form of the Message that Failed as follows: 'God sent the chameleon to mankind with the message that they should have eternal life, and the lizard with the message that they must die. The chameleon dawdled on the way, and the lizard arrived first. When she had delivered her message, the matter was settled. The chameleon's message was no longer valid, and death had entered the world.'

70   *co-wife*: hostility between co-wives is a common theme in African oral literature. In this version of the Sunjata epic co-wife hostility is not prominent, but it is considerably more prominent in other versions. In D. T. Niane (1965), for example, the senior co-wife of Sunjata's mother is constantly plotting to secure and keep the kingship for her own son, at the expense of Sunjata.

71   Notice that the second messenger is a griot, whereas the first messenger was a slave. As will be seen in the next few lines, the griot delivered his message immediately, before the slave, who had sat down to eat first. It seems probable that the opportunity is being taken here to make a little propaganda in favour of griots.

75   *Naareng Daniyang Konnate*: here a term of address to Sunjata's father, whose name was Fata Kung Makhang. When Bamba Suso was asked to explain the name Naareng Daniyang Konnate, he said that Naareng was the name of Sunjata's father's town (Naarena), that Daniyang Konnate was a praise name and Konnate the family name. It was common practice for the name of the king's town or territory to precede the name of the king (e.g. Sankarang Madiba Konte, 'Madiba Konte of Sankarang'). A very common line in Sunjata's praises is 'Simbong ning Jata be Naarena', 'The Master-Hunter and the Lion are at Naarena'. The location of the capital of Manding has been the subject of much scholarly debate, but it seems probable that the

search for *the* capital is a search for something that did not exist. It is unlikely that there was one town which was the permanent site of government; the king of Mali seems to have moved around his territory, not to have settled permanently in one place, so Bamba Suso is probably nearer the truth, when he lists several towns as Sunjata's towns, than are those who press the exclusive claims of any single town. Bamba Suso mentioned Kirina and Kaaba as also being Sunjata's towns, but Naarena, according to him, was Sunjata's town at the time when he became widely known to griots.

82–4   Bamba Suso seems to be suggesting here that Sunjata was so angry that his younger brother had been recognized as the firstborn son that he refused to walk for seven years. Griots generally do not suggest any reason for Sunjata's lameness.

86   Boys were usually circumcised when they were in their teens, and immediately after circumcision they underwent a period of training in seclusion in the bush. A boy is a trainee from the time that he is selected as a candidate for circumcision until he leaves the training area.

101–21   In both versions of the Sunjata epic presented here, it is made clear that despite his unpromising start in life Sunjata was always destined to defeat Sumanguru and to make himself master of Manding. The various techniques by which the young Sunjata was identified as the future ruler of Manding are described in some detail.

130   This statement about the behaviour of griots reflects the very widely held view that griots are attracted to persons of wealth and will leave a patron who falls on hard times.

136–41   The griots apparently decided that they would not immediately abandon Sunjata, but that if he failed to provide for them – and they were sure that he would so fail – then they would bring about his death by mentioning the names of the three hairs. After Sunjata's death, they would be able to go to some wealthy patrons, without arousing any adverse criticism at their having deserted Sunjata. No information is available on the three hairs: to mention their names brings death; but the belief does seem related to two common, present-day beliefs. The first is the belief in the power of a name. It recalls the secret names of God, known only to a very few Islamic scholars. The use of these secret names in extreme circumstances could ensure that God would bring about the desired end requested by the petitioner. The second belief is one current among the Gambian Mandinka, that every member of any particular family is born with some specific physical feature which marks him as a member of that family.

147   *scorn*: denotes the reaction of a griot to a gift which he considers inadequate. As well as disparaging remarks, this involves expressive body movements and facial expressions. Griots are adept at conveying a feeling of amazement tinged with contempt that a man could be so utterly lacking in *savoir-faire*, so mean, so poverty-stricken, that he could give a griot such a contemptible little gift. A man who has been the object of a griot's praises will often give the griot more than he would really like to because of the fear that a smaller sum might provoke a 'scorn' reaction from the griot. Such a reaction would publicly humiliate the person aimed at.

149   Part of Sunjata's praises. Praises commonly refer to some outstanding incident in the life of the praised person. Here, 'Bee, little bee' refers to the incident when Sunjata went into the bush and collected honey to give to his griots. Makhara Makhang Konnate is Sunjata, whose family name was originally Konnate. Bamba Suso was able to offer no explanation of the names Haimaru and Yammaru other than that they were praise names, applied only to Sunjata.

154   This line is part of Sunjata's praises; *Simbong* means 'Master-hunter' in eastern Mande languages, see note on line 75.

160   This line is part of Sunjata's praises; *jato faata lambe la* means 'the lion is full of dignity'; Innes's translation renders the line as 'the lion has its fill of followers' because he was perhaps uncertain of the meaning of the Eastern Mande word *lambe*.

162   *strip of cloth*: cloth is woven in a narrow strip and this long strip is then cut up into lengths which are sewn together to make a *faano*, a 'cloth' or 'pagne' (as it is usually called in Gambian English).

169   The etymology of the name Sunjata which Bamba Suso is giving here is *sung*, 'thief' and *jata*, 'lion'.

184   *korte*: a 'medicine' used in sorcery. It is used both to protect the owner and to attack his enemies, as well as in divination. Certain roots are used in the preparation of *korte*, which comes in different forms but is usually a powder and often kept in a horn (*bino*). Important families mostly had a *korte* horn, which was passed down from generation to generation within the family. The *korte* horn would be consulted when difficulties arose and its advice sought. The owner of the *korte* horn would normally employ it to attack someone only if that person had grievously harmed him or his family; the power of the *korte* was not lightly unleashed. *Korte* could be administered

in several different ways; for example, some could be put under a fingernail and flicked in the direction of the victim, or the owner might wash in water to which some *korte* powder has been added, and then show himself to his victim.

192   Many of the heroes of Mandinka oral tradition are said to have been hunters; elephant hunting seems to have been particularly prestigious.

195   It was the usual practice for a hunter to cut off the tail of an animal he had killed but which was too heavy for him to carry home. Possession of the tail was accepted as proof that it was he who had killed it, and it thus provided proof of ownership of the carcass. When Sunjata gave the *korte* men the tail (204–6), he was in fact handing over ownership of the carcass. It was of course the elephant which Sunjata said that they should add to their meat, not the tail.

214   This is a common saying; it implies that God alone determines when a man is to die.

216   *he could hinder the fulfilment of your destiny*: in Islamic belief a man's life is predestined and nothing can alter what God has ordained. In pre-Islamic Mandinka belief, on the other hand, sorcery could be employed to bring about desired ends, such as the injury or death of an enemy. Clearly here there is a conflict of irreconcilable beliefs, and apparently some sort of reconciliation is attempted: although what is predestined cannot be altered, at least its fulfilment can be delayed. This doctrine that predestined events can be delayed, although not averted, is not part of orthodox Islamic belief.

220   *Kutuma*: the precise meaning of this word is uncertain; it may be either 'hunchback' or 'covered in boils/carbuncles', though the latter would be the more likely meaning in Gambian Mandinka.

222   See note on line 75.

225   There is some disagreement among griots about the name of Sunjata's sister. According to Banna Kanute, her name was Nene Faamaga.

226   *horn*: it is not clear exactly what kind of horn is meant here. It may well be a *korte* horn (see note on line 184), for Sunjata was himself skilled in the magical arts.

238   According to Bamba Suso, Tamaga Jonding Keya's town was called Taabu. This can probably be identified with Tabon, mentioned by D. T. Niane (1965) as a town in Futa Jallon where Sunjata and his mother had hospitality for some time before they went on to Wagadu in the old empire of Ghana, and then to Neema (Mema in French). However, in Niane's version the king of Tabon was a Kamara, whereas in Bamba's version, he is a Darbo.

239   The Darbos are one of the *jula* (trader) families, and also one of the leading families in the Gambia.

250–55   Here the ordeal of removing a ring from a pot of boiling wax is used as a means of identifying the person who was destined to become king of Manding. This sort of ordeal is more commonly used in trials to determine guilt or innocence.

256   *declaration*: involves a public statement, usually about one's status or one's prowess in some activity, with a challenge to anyone to disprove the claim which is made. At the present day a man may challenge his companions to a competition, and this challenge will be announced by a drummer who will accompany the announcement of the challenge with a particular tune. For example, when several young men are engaged in hoeing a groundnut farm, one of them may tell the drummer to announce that he declares that he can plough without a break for longer than any of the others. Several of the young men can be expected to take up the challenge, and they will then all compete to see whether the challenger can substantiate his claim.

270   *freeborn*: Mandinka society is divided into three strata: the freeborn (nobility), descendants of slaves and occupational groups. Innes originally translates as 'freeman'.

279–81   The declaration that during the whole of her seven years' pregnancy his mother had never had a fright is really saying that his mother had been an ideal wife who had never given her husband occasion to speak sharply to her. It is also an indirect boast about Sunjata's own character since it is believed that the behaviour of the mother is reflected in the career of her sons. See also note on line 50.

284   Sunjata draws his knife and threatens to kill his mother (288). These lines would be highly charged with emotion for a Mandinka man and his mother, and in Sunjata's case the relationship was particularly close. This is apparent from many incidents in Bamba's narration; for example, when Sunjata was still a cripple and had made unsuccessful attempts to rise up with the aid of crutches, he then called his mother and rose to his feet with her aid. Again, she accompanied him on all his wanderings in exile and when he was summoned to return to Manding to take up the kingship, Sunjata refused to go until his mother, who was then ill, either died and was properly buried or else recovered and was able to travel with him. For Sunjata to turn on his mother and threaten her with a knife reflects the extreme anguish he felt when he suspected that he might not be legitimate.

This suspicion drove him so frantic that he threatened his mother's life if she did not tell him the truth about his birth.

289   *maga*: the meaning is obscure but it probably denotes some big animal.

292   Maabirama Konnate was Sunjata's paternal uncle, according to Bamba. In reciting someone's praises, griots mention the names of any of his famous relatives, and this is presumably why Maabirama Konnate is mentioned.

298–307   These lines show Sunjata's great concern for the fate of his griots after his death. They warn the people of today to be generous to their griots.

318   *I had made my boast*: refers to Sunjata's declaration in lines 279–81 that if it were the case that his mother had been pregnant with him for seven years and had never in all that time had a sudden fright, then the tree should fall down when he shot it.

346   It is not certain why the soothsayer should have warned Sunjata against retaliating when provoked, but it probably reflects the Mandinka belief that patience and self-restraint are virtues, and that a man destined for leadership should learn self-control.

357   *kill by witchcraft*: a witch is believed to be able to remove the victim's *nio* (vital principle, the immaterial part of a man's make-up) from his body and to hang it up somewhere, often on a tree. When the *nio* shrivels up, the victim dies. All the griots' versions agree that Sumanguru was a master of the occult arts. Sunjata too was skilled in this field, though not so highly skilled as Sumanguru. The fighting between Sunjata and Sumanguru was carried on at the supernatural level as well as at the mundane level of the battlefield. Sumanguru could never be overcome purely by military means.

359–60   These two lines seem to be an echo of part of the praises of Faa Ganda (Sunjata's maternal grandfather): 'Faa Ganda killed his in-law on Monday,/Next Monday Faa Ganda came into power.'

386   The bestowing of family names is attributed to Sunjata, who is said to have given names which recalled some event in the recipient's life. The etymology which Bamba Suso has in mind is not stated clearly, but from the context it seems likely that he takes Fofana to consist of *foo*, 'miss' or 'lose' and *fana*, 'also' (= *fanang*). This fits well with line 385, where Sunjata tells his brother that he (the brother) has missed any chance of becoming king of Manding. It is not clear why Sunjata was so severe on his younger brother for having greeted his sister so enthusiastically, but it is possible that he may have

suspected incest. Sunjata is said to have arrived to find his brother and sister on the ground together.

400–436   The incident of the king of Neema's demand for payment for the burial plot and Sunjata's reply is found in many versions of the epic. The account in Niane (1965) is similar to the one here, except that in Niane the king of Neema refuses Sunjata permission to bury his mother because he was angry at Sunjata's decision to return to Manding. The king of Neema had instructed Sunjata in the military arts and had hoped that he would one day be his successor. Angered at what he regarded as Sunjata's desertion, he at first ordered Sunjata to take his mother's corpse to Manding with him, but then allowed him to bury her, provided that he paid for the burial plot.

404–7   Sunjata has to join gold earrings together in a chain which will stretch from her head to her feet and then to lay this chain on the ground. The length of the chain will be the length of the burial plot. The chain of earrings will be the payment which Sunjata has to make.

446   The incident in which a man cuts off part of his leg to provide for his starving companion is common not only among the Mandinka but also among neighbouring peoples such as the Wolof and Fula. A variety of different characters are found playing the roles here attributed to Sunjata and his griot. This incident is often given as an account of the origin of the griots and their relationship to their patron families.

449   *kuna fito*: not known.

470   *special relationship*: (*dankuto*) between two lineages in which the members of each group are licensed to tease or jokingly insult each other without any offence being taken. In every case the relationship is said to have originated when a member (or members) of one group helped the other group in some major crisis.

471   The Kuyates are the griots of the Keitas.

476   *Dakhajala*: recent scholarship has established this as the probable 'capital' of Manding (Conrad 1994).

480   This line suggests that the griot did know what a horse was, but that he had never encountered such an animal in Manding or in Neema. There is a strong tradition that Sunjata sent a force to the west to obtain horses, indicating that the west was more of a horse-raising area than the east. The text implies that horses were comparatively rare in Manding in Sunjata's time, but this does not agree very well with Banna Kanute's statement (868–9) that when Sunjata was due

to go for circumcision, every boy who attended the ceremony was mounted on a horse.

483–502 This passage in praise of horses is one of the classic Mande praise songs. By 'call the horses' the griot implies that the individual being praised is descended from a king, since only kings rode horses. The text consists of a string of epithets reflecting qualities of bravery, stoicism and might.

486 *Being dragged*: Bamba Suso's explanation is that if a lion is killed and then dragged over the ground, this will not distress it, as it has often done the same to other animals. Likewise, a king should not be distressed if another king does to him what he himself has done to another.

511 The colour of this kind of horse (*sambango*) is uncertain, but it was perhaps brownish, and it had a white circle on its forehead. It was said to have particularly strong bones. It was believed that a man who went to war mounted on a horse which had a white right foreleg and a white left hind leg would not perish in the war. There is a tradition that a *sambango* was the first horse that Sunjata rode.

517 *army commanders*: high-ranking men who had their own body of armed men and who would bring them to the support of the king when called upon to do so.

520 *Kurang karang*: an ideophone denoting the sound of clanking metal.

521–3 These lines are the praises of Kama Fofana. As the arrival of the various military commanders is mentioned, the name of each of them is followed by his praises.

522 No explanation is available for 'iron shoe', but it seems likely that the phrase refers to some sort of armoured footwear.

524 The number 1,444 is repeated several times as the number of soldiers brought by each commander. Whatever significance this number had in the past has now been lost as far as the Gambian Mandinka are concerned. The same number occurs in Niane's (1960) account of the founding of the famous *kamablon/kamablō* at Kaaba: 'Mansa Souleymane returned from Mecca with 1,444 fetishes, which he lodged in the *kamablō*.'

527 *Tira Makhang*: Sunjata's greatest commander. He is particularly prominent in the traditions current in the Gambia because, after the defeat of Sumanguru, Tira Makhang is said to have come west, reached the valley of the Gambia, and also to have founded Kaabu (in present-day Guinea Bissau).

530–33 Praises of Suru Bande Makhang Kamara. A man's praises very often include the names of famous kinsmen, but in this case, the praises consist of nothing but a list of such names.

540–47   Praises of Sankarang Madiba Konte, also known as Faa Ganda. *Wuruwarang* is an ideophone describing vines intertwined with each other and twining around the branches of the host tree; *kaaba* is a species of tree. The phrase *wuruwarang kaaba* may convey the idea that anyone who came into conflict with Sankarang Madiba Konte would never escape from him.

556–8   The meaning appears to be that Tira Makhang can fight from morning till night and still be able to join in a great battle.

565   The navel is regarded as a particularly vulnerable part of the body; children are warned that if they play with their navels they are likely to die. For the Fula, see note on line 446.

576   There is some uncertainty about the significance of the red arrow. It may refer to an arrow which was tipped with a red poisonous substance, and at line 838 it does seem that the tip of the arrow was covered with a red substance (see note on line 838). On the other hand, Bamba Suso stated in discussion of this phrase that each commander had weapons of a distinctive colour so that after a battle it would be possible to determine whose arrow had killed whom.

578   Susu Sumanguru's father was a seven-headed jinn who lived in a hill. Sumanguru was invulnerable and invincible so long as his father remained alive, and his father could only be killed by an arrow tipped with the spur of a white cock. This has significance later in the story.

582   This is a commonplace of griots' recitations; cf. line 499: 'many great matters have passed from the world'.

585   There are no heroic figures left in the world now; all the great men are dead. This is a common theme in griots' performances. They constantly refer to the great figures of the past who knew how to behave nobly, in particular how to treat griots properly, and they bewail the fact that things are changed now and that there are no longer such great men. It is a commonplace of griots' recitations that the world has changed for the worse, and certainly, as far as the position of the Mandinka griots themselves is concerned, this is true.

587   *youthful king*: great men die young; men who distinguished themselves by their bravery in battle were usually killed before they reached old age.

589   See note on line 75.

593   Anachronistic reference to the nineteenth-century Muslim leader, al-Hajj 'Umar Tal. He waged holy war throughout the Mande-

speaking area and is remembered in song by the griots. He died in 1864.

599–605 Praises of Faa Koli Dumbuya who was Sumanguru's nephew: Sora Musa, 'Musa the piercer'; Kiliya Musa, 'Musa the jealous'; Nooya Musa, 'Musa the able'; also sometimes Faa Koli Kumba ning Faa Koli Daaba, 'Faa Koli the big head and the big mouth'. Although not included in this performance it is well known that Faa Koli joined forces with Sunjata against Sumanguru, after the latter had stolen Faa Koli's wife.

605 *eye red as Bureng gold*: people with reddish whites of the eye are thought to be fierce and aggressive (those whose white of eye is very white are thought to be mild, gentle, unaggressive). Buré is an area in the extreme north-east of Guinea, famous for its goldfields. The goldfields of Buré were one of the principal sources of the gold for which the Sudan had such a reputation among Europeans in the Middle Ages, especially after the pilgrimage of Mansa Musa, Emperor of Mali (1307–32) who is reputed to have taken some 50,000 ounces of gold with him, much of which he distributed in gifts and alms.

616–36 In this passage Bamba Suso is indicating the crucial role that Sunjata's general Tira Makhang played in establishing the main lineages in the Senegambia. He links current surnames, such as Job and Juf, to Tira Makhang. Another version of the name Tira Makhang is Taraware, which is the present-day Traoré.

643 *Kirikisa*: the meaning is obscure.

670 There is widespread agreement among griots that Kankinyang was the site of a bitter, but inconclusive, engagement between Sunjata and Sumanguru. Griots sing a song commemorating the battle of Kankinyang; D. T. Niane (1965) gives a version of the song: 'The battle of Kankigne was terrible;/Men were less dignified than slaves there.'

Banna Kanute quotes another version of this song, see lines 1980–83. As will be seen from Bamba Suso's lines 675 ff., Sunjata's griots thought that Sunjata was afraid, and Niane says, 'there had been great fear in Djata's ranks'.

674 *did this*: he shook it.

677 *Kubang Kubang*: an ideophone, 'slow runner'; in this context the implication is that Sunjata runs slowly because he is not afraid. Bamba Suso explained this by saying that it occurs in Eastern Manding, corresponding in meaning to Gambian Mandinka *yofu-yofu*, 'to run slowly'. He also explained that Sunjata's griot did not wish the word

to get about that Sunjata had run when Sumanguru fired an arrow at him, and, in order to forestall any such adverse report, the griot made up a praise name for Sunjata referring to the incident.

681   *Dendending*: the meaning is obscure.

691   This line is a common saying; it means that a person who has been going on at something without really thinking about it, and relying on brute force, is only made aware of his foolishness when something untoward happens; for example, when a man who is in the habit of beating his wife is arrested one day for assaulting her. Perhaps in relation to Sunjata it is intended to mean that until they have come up against Sunjata and been severely dealt with by him, other men did not realize how inferior they were.

694-5   These lines mean that there is more than one way of doing a thing, and that one can achieve one's aim by stealth as well as by brute force.

696   *the smith*: Sumanguru, who was a blacksmith, one of the occupational groups.

704-7   Praises of smiths; here each of the four phrases was the name of one of the gates leading into Sumanguru's town. *Kuku* is a tall tree with edible fruit. Smiths sometimes have their forges under such a tree, and this is probably why it is mentioned in smiths' praises. Likewise with the silk-cotton tree.

706   *Push-in-front Expert*: from the action of the smith in pushing forward on the anvil the piece of metal to be struck with the hammer.

707   *Lift the Hammer*: this phrase is probably parallel to the phrase in line 706, but with 'expert' not repeated, i.e. 'hammer-lifting (expert)'.

709   *gateways*: bulungo is a gateway or gatehouse, rectangular in plan, with a gate at each end and a roof over it. Sometimes men sit in it in order to chat with people passing through. In the traditional Mandinka compound, which was surrounded by a wall, the entrance passed through the house of the compound owner, who could thus keep an eye on everyone entering or leaving the compound.

722   Mandinka etiquette requires that when someone visits him, the person visited give the visitor a small gift.

725-6   Marriage, or sexual intercourse, between freeborn and occupational groups, such as blacksmiths, was prohibited. Even today in the Gambia there is opposition to such unions, though they do sometimes happen.

728   The smith's thoughts turned to having sexual intercourse with the woman.

740   The tradition that Sumanguru had two mothers does not seem to be

very widespread among the griots. It does not occur in the published versions. The motif of the child with more than one mother is extremely rare in oral literature.

742   *Susuo*: the ethnic group Susu (Sosso) to which Sumanguru belonged. The Susu are found principally in Guinea and are distant linguistic relatives of the Mande.

752   *these events*: the visit of Sunjata's sister to Sumanguru.

772   Robert Pageard (1961) has suggested that the cock's spur may symbolize virility; wild guinea-corn may symbolize fertility. In Niane (1965) it is Sunjata who fires the arrow, and though this merely grazes Sumanguru, he immediately 'felt his powers leave him'. In Bamba Suso's version, Sumanguru loses all his strength as soon as his father is shot by the arrow. Clearly then, the arrow does not operate against Sumanguru on the physical plane; it operates by depriving him of all his vital powers; it attacks his virility, his power of creation.

788   Sumanguru broke off in the middle of the word *jambatutuo*, 'Senegalese coucal'. This bird is very common in the Gambia, where it is believed that it is not good to shoot it, though the reason for this belief is not generally known; cf. lines 796–7. The fact that Sumanguru broke off in the middle of the word is very important, as will be seen later in the story.

834   *Kante family*: Sumanguru belonged to the Kante lineage. For one version of the etymology of the name Kante, see Banna Kanute, line 1343 and note.

838   *mananda*: the meaning is obscure, which is unfortunate as it is the key to our understanding of why Sankarang Madiba Konte was called 'Firer of the red arrow'; see note on line 576.

847–8   The meaning is that if Sunjata's forces managed to find and kill Sumanguru, then the latter's leaderless army would be of no consequence as a fighting force.

859–60   Notice that Sumanguru is not killed but disappears in the shape of a bird into thick bush. Likewise in Niane (1965), Sumanguru eludes Sunjata by disappearing into a cave. After his father had been killed, Sumanguru tried to elude Sunjata's soldiers by changing into various objects he had mentioned to Sunjata's sister (lines 782–6), but she recognized him in each new shape and sent the troops after him. But when he changed into a Senegalese coucal, she failed to recognize him, as he had stopped short halfway through telling her that this was one of the shapes that he would change into (788). Unrecognized as a coucal, Sumanguru flew off and escaped from Sunjata.

861–8   Praises of Sumanguru linked to the tools and techniques of smiths. *Manda* (Gambian Mandinka: *tunkango*), 'anvil'; *Saamagha*, meaning obscure; *Tunkang*, 'to forge' or 'an anvil'; *Baayang*, 'pincers'; *Sege* (Gambian Mandinka: *see*), 'cut'.

884   *Dango*: (Gambian Mandinka: *sio*) the meaning is uncertain, but is most probably 'rhinoceros'. The word *sio* occurs only in stories, not in ordinary speech. Informants agree that it refers to a big animal that existed in the past, but which no longer exists, at least not in the Gambia; informants have little idea what the animal looked alike.

890–91   *Damfa*: the etymology of the name which Bamba Suso is proposing here is *dang*, 'rhinoceros' and *fagha*, 'kill'.

892–5   *Danso*: the etymology proposed for the name is *sira*, 'road' and *sogho*, 'pierce' or 'thrust through'.

897   *kenyeramatigi*: the meaning is obscure.

904   *Tamaga Jonding Keya*: first gave Sunjata shelter when he was forced to leave Manding. Later he became jealous of Sunjata and refused to let him remain, so Sunjata left and went to stay at Neema; see lines 237ff.

    Darbo: the etymology for the name proposed by Bamba Suso is *daa*, 'mouth' and *bo*, 'remove' = *Daa bo*, 'withdraw from some matter' or 'give up an involvement in something'.

907   Soora Musa is a praise name of Faa Koli, Sumanguru's nephew, but there is no mention elsewhere of his ever having ruled Manding; see note on lines 599–605.

911   *Tabaski*: Id el Kabir, known in Senegambia as Tabaski. It is an occasion when sheep are sacrificed and considerable expense involved, and a rich man can make a display of his wealth.

913   Bamba Suso made a slip here. As remarked in the note on lines 859–60, Sumanguru is not killed either in Bamba's version or in Niane (1965). When asked later whether Sumanguru was killed, Bamba Suso said no.

Banna Kanute: Sunjata

27   *Dala Kumbukamba . . . Dala Jiibaa Minna*: these do not appear to be the names of actual persons. It is quite common to find such names connoting personal characteristics in griots' narratives. Fanciful names of ancestors occur also in Bamba Suso's narration, for example lines 637–40, where Tira Makhang is said to be descended from Fire, Flame

and Charcoal. The interpretation of the name Dala Kumbukamba is uncertain; *dala* here is perhaps to be identified with *dala*, 'pool' or 'area of water', hence may refer to the sound of liquid swilling about in a container, in this case the sound of palm-wine inside a gourd. Jiibaa Minna means, literally, 'water-big drinker', i.e. a big palm-wine drinker.

32   Dugu and Faabaga Ning Taulajo are the standard praise names for all Kontes.

33–6   These lines are ambiguous: 'he fathered' (36) may refer to Naareng Makhang Konnate (34), but the statement that he had twelve sons does not accord with the statement (43) that Sunjata's mother had borne forty sons by her husband before Sunjata was born. On the other hand, the passage may be a false start, with a syntactic break after Konnate; in that case, 'their' (35) might refer simply to the lineage members and the twelve sons might refer to the founders of the twelve clans of Manding (50). The use of numbers in epic traditions is often symbolic rather than literal. There is a strong tradition that Sunjata's eleven older brothers were killed by Sumanguru, and it is possible that Banna Kanute is conflating that tradition with the one about the forty brothers killed fighting for the Prophet.

35   The ward or section (Mandinka: *kaabilo*) consists of a number of compounds, most of which are contiguous, but it quite often happens that some compounds belonging to a particular ward are scattered in other parts of the village. This situation usually results when members of a section who wish to build their own compounds have found that there was no space available within their section. The section is based on a patrilineage, but it includes also wives, and people (and their descendants) from elsewhere who have attached themselves to the lineage, descendants of slaves and also associated caste members.

45   *Mansa Farang Tunkara*: in several versions of the epic, he is the king of Neema (Mema in the French texts), where Sunjata spent some time while he was in exile. *Mansa*, 'king'; *farang*, 'client king'.

46   *ancestor*: (Malinka: *bemba* or *mbemba*) literally, refers to the reputed founder of a social group such as a lineage or an occupational group. The social hierarchy of the Mande people is said by the griots to have been established by Sunjata; the founders of the clans were therefore contemporaries of Sunjata.

48   Sumanguru was a smith by birth. Normally a member of an occupational group could not be king. Compare also lines 1570–71, where Sunjata's sister declares that Sumanguru would never have sexual

intercourse with her because she was a princess and he a smith. The prohibition on marriage between freeborn and members of occupational groups is still widely observed in the Gambia.

50–58   With the twelve sections/wards (see note on line 35) mentioned here, compare 'the twelve doors of Manding' in Niane (1965), said to 'refer to the twelve provinces of which Mali was originally composed'. The Jaane, Komma, Ture, Siise (and Berete) are the five lineages described as the five original Muslim families of Mande. The implication is that these lineages did not seek political power.

75   *marabouts*: religious clerics, sometimes holy men.

76–8   Diviners employing a variety of techniques: *kuurung*, 'cowrie shell' is a technique based on the relative number of shells which fall with the concave or convex side uppermost when thrown on the ground; *bere*, 'stone' is a technique based on patterns made by small stones dropped on the ground; *kenye*, 'sand' is a technique based on patterns drawn in fine sand.

83   It is not uncommon for the leading lineage to claim descent from an ancestor who had some link with the Prophet or with one of the Companions of the Prophet. But in the Gambia it is not usual for griots to make any mention of such a link in the case of Sunjata; in fact, of several versions collected there, this was the only one to mention such a connection. As will be seen later, Islam is more than usually prominent in this version. Haibara (Khaibar) is an oasis in Saudi Arabia about a hundred miles north of Medina. In AD 628 the Prophet led an army against the Jewish settlement at Khaibar; after six weeks' siege and some heavy fighting he captured it, and the Jews were forced to pay an annual tribute of half their harvest.

89   *Sorakhata*: according to a widespread tradition, he was a Companion of the Prophet and an ancestor of the griots.

116–20   These five lines are part of Sunjata's praises, and they occur repeatedly throughout the narration, see Bamba Suso, note on line 75.

116   *Sukulung Kutuma*: Sunjata's mother; *kutu* means 'protrusion', so *kutuma* may mean 'with bumps, carbuncles, warts', or 'hunchbacked', though this latter meaning is unlikely in Gambian Mandinka.

117   *Sukulung Yammaru*: according to Bamba Suso, Sunjata himself, but this is by no means certain; it was, and still is, common for the mother's name to occur as part of the son's name. Another explanation which is sometimes given is that this is the name of another Sukulung, and when Sunjata's father went to the place advised by the diviners he was first offered Sukulung Yammaru, but he refused her and chose

Sukulung Kutuma, again as advised by the diviners, despite her ugliness. The meaning of Yammaru is obscure.

118 *Naareng Makhang Konnate*: there is some disagreement among griots on whether this name refers to Sunjata or to his father, or both. According to Banna Kanute (33–4), this is the name of Sunjata's father, but Bamba Suso states (178–9) that it was Sunjata's name and that his father's name was Fata Kung Makhang. It seems probable in fact that the name could be used for both Sunjata and his father.

119 This commemorates an incident in Sunjata's life shortly after his father died; when his griots attended upon him, Sunjata had nothing to give them, so he went and seized a cat, carried it back slung over his shoulder and presented it to his griots, see Bamba Suso, lines 152–4.

120 *Simbong*: see Bamba Suso, note on line 154.

130 In a Mandinka polygynous household, the husband and his wives have separate sleeping quarters; each wife takes it in turn to sleep in the husband's house.

131–46 These lines are a digression by Banna Kanute to signal a change of melodic accompaniment: he is now playing the tune associated with Faa Koli Dumbuya (see note on line 1993).

133 Sunjata's most fearsome general, Faa Koli, was the son of Sumanguru's sister, Kumba Kante. The griots often say that his father was a jinn called Musa. Faa Koli has many praise names which capture elements of the story of his defection to Sunjata's side. He was brought up by his uncle Sumanguru, and trained in the art of war, but later Sumanguru desired Faa Koli's wife, since she was more beautiful than all of his own hundred wives. Sumanguru then stole Faa Koli's wife. The name of the town in which Sumanguru announced to his nephew that he was taking his wife from him was Kiliya (meaning 'jealousy'). Faa Koli went off in anger and founded a town of his own called Nooya ('ability'), and joined forces with Sunjata against his uncle. Faa Koli became one of Sunjata's greatest military commanders. He is called *Kumba* because he was said to have a large head and metaphorically someone with a big head has powers to see what is hidden from ordinary men. He is also *Daaba*, meaning, 'big mouth, braggart'. These two epithets are always linked with 'and', but refer only to the one Faa Koli (cf. Simbong and Jata, and Bamba Suso, note on line 75).

141 *Tuluku Muluku*: an ideophone, 'of being oily' or 'slippery'. Here it refers to the ease with which the spear goes through flesh.

149–63   Sorakhata precedes his important message with standard praise names of the Kontes and of Sunjata.

176   *rak'a*: a unit of Muslim ritual prayer.

186–7   The griots are agreed that Sunjata's sister accompanied him into exile and played the vital part of discovering the secret of Sumanguru's invulnerability and invincibility, but they are not agreed on the sister's name. Banna Kanute calls her Nene Faamaga, Bamba Suso calls her Nyakhaleng Juma Suukho; Niane (1965) states that the sister who discovered Sumanguru's secret was Sunjata's half-sister, Nana Triban, and that he had two full sisters, Sogolon Kolonkan and Sogolon Djamarou (francophone spelling of Sukulung Yammaru).

213–17   Praises referring to Faa Koli Dumbuya.

245–6   This is one of the well-known songs associated with Sunjata.

263   *Running away*: This refers to an incident when Sunjata was seen running during a battle with Sumanguru. In order to prevent any adverse reports of the incident getting about, Sunjata's griots made up a *too dimang*, a 'fine name' or 'pleasant name' to commemorate the incident. The name was Kubang Kubang, see Bamba Suso, note on line 676.

265   The Siise lineage is one of the five holy families who first converted to Islam (see note on lines 50–58), and who commonly have the phrase *Manding Moori*, 'Manding Muslim' attached to the lineage name.

277–83   Sumanguru's praise names; most of them have some reference to blacksmithing, see lines 1952–63 for Banna Kanute's own explanations.

277   *Sirimang*: a nickname for a smith and also for a billygoat – smiths have a reputation for sexual prowess.

278   *the left hand*: probably a reference to the use of the left hand for holding (with pincers) the piece of metal which is being hammered into shape.

279   *Senegalese coucal*: see Bamba Suso, note on line 788.

281   The ability to shatter other swords makes a sword particularly valuable or highly prized.

282   Smiths often work in the shade of a big tree, hence these two are associated with smiths.

283   No explanation has been found for this line except that given by Banna Kanute in line 1963.

287   The concept of seven layers of sky and seven layers of earth was probably part of pre-Islamic Manding cosmology.

295–6   Unintelligible except for isolated Arabic words.

320–22   A theme which frequently recurs in griots' recitations is that in the past people knew how to treat them properly, but now things have changed for the worse.

380–81   For Banna Kanute's version of the etymology of the name Kante, see lines 1323–9 and 1940–42.

459–61   Unintelligible except for isolated Arabic words.

463   God had ordained Sunjata's kingship.

485   The Yalunke (spelt variously Dyalonke, Yalonka, Jalonke, Yalunke, Djallonke) are a section of the Susu ethnic group in Futa Jallon, Guinea.

506   The Mandinka *koma* is a masked figure which appears at night, usually when a town is threatened or has suffered an unexplained series of misfortunes, such as the deaths of several children. Smiths are responsible for preparing the masquerader and arranging his appearance.

508–10   These three lines are repeated frequently in griots' narrations, with the appropriate name occurring where here we have Susu Sumanguru Baamagana.

509   *cold*: dead.

613   *steamer*: a kind of earthenware colander with holes in it used for steaming millet flour.

630–34   When Sunjata's mother had pounded millet for someone, she received as payment the hard pieces which could not be made into flour, and softened them by steaming.

681   *it was named*: the naming ceremony occurs on the seventh day after a child is born. If the child dies before then, it is believed not to have fully entered the world.

719   An anachronism as Sunjata is already twelve years old in this version.

753   Sunjata was born with the surname Konnate, but he was given a new surname Keita meaning 'take your inheritance'. He was thus the first of the Keita line.

761–2   The meaning is obscure but they are praise names probably reflecting the esoteric power of the Kontes.

774   The implication here is that although he was twelve years of age, Sunjata still spent his time with the women and babies, and was therefore not a grown-up man.

796–8   These lines are unintelligible.

800   Banna Kanute does not in fact refer to these lines again.

810–17   Faa Koli's praises.

818–19   Praises of Jinna Musa, Faa Koli's father.

842–3   According to other Gambian griots, Mansa Farang Tunkara had his capital at Neema, located by D. T. Niane some fifty miles down-river from Mopti on the Niger. There is some disagreement among scholars as to the exact location of Neema.

842   *Serahuli*: (also spelt Sarakolle or Serehulle) a Mande ethnic group, also known as Soninke and Maraka.

862–3   It had been prophesied that whoever swallowed a seed of the baobab fruit would rule in Manding for sixty years; see lines 75–80.

956   The meaning is obscure. In Gambian Mandinka *simbaro* means 'a big baboon'.

979   *korte*: see Bamba Suso, note on line 184.

1037   *He*: Sunjata.

1082   *Ni wadi*: this has no meaning for Gambian Mandinka speakers, as Banna Kanute doubtless realized, since he explains it in the next line.

1133–4   These two lines suggest that both names, Sukulung Kutuma and Sukulung Yammaru, refer to Sunjata's mother. Bamba Suso, on the other hand, stated that Sukulung Yammaru in his narrative refers to Sunjata himself.

1185   *naso*: a liquid prepared by marabouts by writing verses in black ink from the Koran on a wooden writing board and then washing these off. *Naso* is believed to have magical properties and is widely used to this day.

1188   *bisimalato*: probably 'Bismillahi', the opening phrase of prayer, one written on the writing board and then washed off in the preparation of *naso*.

1192   *special ingredients*: any substance (for example a pinch of sand, a hair) which a marabout prescribes must be added to the material which he has prepared. A marabout who has prepared a piece of paper for incorporation in an amulet will also prescribe the *sumareo*, 'special ingredient' which must be included. The leather amulet itself will be made by a leatherworker, who will enclose the piece of paper and the *sumareo* in the leather holder.

1323   *I didn't say anything*: (literally, 'it was not my voice') is a translation of the Mandinka *n kang te*. The pun on the name Kante implies both a fearfulness on the part of Sumanguru and an etymology for his name. In lines 1322–9 Banna Kanute is making sure that his audience will appreciate the point. According to Banna Kanute, Sumanguru's surname was Baamagana (which may be borrowed from Hausa since the phrase in Hausa means 'nothing was said'), but as a result of this incident Sunjata decreed that he should be called Kante (see lines 1343 and 1941–2).

1334 *Urinate*: it is believed that urine can destroy the efficacy of an amulet.

1360–62 Part of one of the best-known songs associated with Sunjata. The lines imply that though others may run to Sunjata for protection, Sunjata does not seek protection from anyone; see lines 1386–95 for a fuller version of this song.

1395 *ding kasi kang*: the meaning is unclear.

1431–4 The reason for the griot's sending Jinna Musa off to Mecca may be simply to explain where the special spear, Tuluku Muluku, came from. But it is just possible that this pilgrimage is a dim memory of the famous pilgrimage of Mansa Musa, which caused such a stir in Europe and the Middle East. Gambian oral tradition seems to be silent on Mansa Musa.

1442 *Baha la nankang*: the meaning is unclear.

1447 *These two people*: seems to refer to Faa Koli Kumba and Faa Koli Daaba, mentioned in the preceding two lines, but these two names are in fact two names for one man, see note on line 133. Throughout his narration Banna Kanute does seem to fluctuate between taking the two names Faa Koli Kumba and Faa Koli Daaba as sometimes referring to one person and sometimes to two.

1494 *the eve of Friday*: some Muslims in the Gambia make a practice of sleeping on the ground instead of in their beds on Thursday night, in preparation for Friday, the prayer day.

1500 This is a proverb meaning 'You have no secrets from me'.

1513 *held his two hands up*: when Faa Koli had raised the iron rod above his head to deliver a blow, his arms locked in that position, preventing him from striking.

1536–64 These lines explain how the griot got his name. Bala is a nickname for Musa, which was his name (1560); *bala* also of course means 'xylophone'. The etymology of Faasigi is given here as *fasa*, 'tendon' and *sigi*, 'settle' or 'live', referring to the fact that Sunjata cut the griot's Achilles tendons so that he could not return to Sumanguru, and then ordered him to settle (*sigi*) at Sunjata's place.

1552–3 The implication is that Bala Faasigi played the xylophone so sweetly that Sunjata did not want him to go back to Manding.

1570 Though Sunjata's sister is prepared to go through a form of marriage with Sumanguru (1569), she will never allow him to have sexual intercourse with her. Marriage or sexual intercourse between a freeborn person and a member of a caste was forbidden.

1588   *raised himself*: from a reclining to a sitting position. Even today, chiefs commonly recline (often on one elbow) on a mat spread on the floor.

1620   *reason*: (*dalila*) can mean 'power to produce an effect on something', 'supernatural power' or 'magical power'.

1620–24 The translation of *dalila/dalilo* in these lines is not always certain, particularly in line 1622, where the phrase *dalila kamma* seems to mean 'on account of some supernatural power', implying that Sunjata's sister feels impelled by some power to marry Sumanguru, though such a marriage is prohibited, as she seems to suggest herself (1621). She appears to be asking Sumanguru to explain to her what this compelling power is, a power which can also kill Sumanguru. At this point in the story the griots have the problem of explaining how it was that Sunjata's sister managed to persuade Sumanguru to reveal to her the secret of his invulnerability. In other versions, Sunjata's sister tells Sumanguru that she needs to know what it is that will harm him so that she can avoid injuring him inadvertently, for example by giving him food to eat which is taboo to him. In all versions, Sumanguru's defences against the woman's wiles are weakened by his desire for her, which she tells him cannot be satisfied till he has told her about his invulnerability.

1640   The implication is that when a woman lies down at a man's back she signals that she submits to him.

1676–80 These lines emphasize that Sunjata's sister is older than he is, probably with the implication that being older and wiser than her brother, Nene Faamaga had discovered how to defeat Sumanguru, something which Sunjata had failed to achieve.

1677   *little mother*: stepmother.

1678   *little father*: paternal uncle.

1690   See note on line 27.

1706   *Bozos*: a fishing people, numbering about 30,000, who live on the banks of the Middle Niger.

1712   See Bamba Suso, note on line 162.

1753   An unintelligible phrase uttered by the sorcerer during consultation.

1790   *Sibi Kamara*: i.e. Kamara of Sibi; Sibi was a town under the control of the Kamaras. It is in south-west Mali, near the Guinea border.

1791–9 The praise names for Sibi Kamara take us down the genealogical trail all the way to the famous nineteenth-century warlord Almami Samori Ture.

1830–31 These lines give a proposed etymology for the name Susokho (variant: Suso): *su*, 'horse' and *soo*, 'spur'.

1883 *double-barrelled gun*: (*daa fulo*) literally, 'two mouths'. This is of course an anomaly; in most versions, the cock's spur is attached to the tip of an arrow, not fired from a gun.

1892–3 *Go ahead*: it is the convention that the inferior of two combatants makes the first move; Sunjata's invitation to Sumanguru to go ahead and make the first move in the fight is contemptuous, since it implies that Sunjata, though the younger of the two, regards himself as Sumanguru's superior.

1895 Sumanguru withdrew a short distance so that he could bear down upon Sunjata at speed.

1914 The context makes it probable that this sentence means it was Sunjata who struck Sumanguru, although the three-pronged spear was mentioned earlier (1887) as one of Sumanguru's weapons.

1954–63 In this passage Banna Kanute explains Sumanguru's praises which consist of various techniques and objects associated with black-smithing. They are also metaphors in which Sunjata and Sumanguru are contrasted: the pincers hold the metal tight (1957); one man gets the better of another (1959); however big a tree is, the space round it is bigger (1961); the funnel of the bellows is kept firmly in place by the mound of baked clay (1963).

1954 *sege*: to cut; it probably refers to the cutting and shaping of metal by smiths.

Sirimang: a nickname for smiths; and see note on line 277.

1962 *Fari* means 'bellows', but *kaunju* does not occur in Gambian Mandinka.

1976–7 The griots say that Manding was destroyed and rebuilt nineteen times.

1993 *Janjungo*: the name of the tune which Banna Kanute has used for most of this performance; *Janjungo* is one of the most important and serious of the griots' repertoire of tunes, only performed for great warriors and their descendants, by older musicians. The word origin-ally means 'hymn to bravery'.

1995 It was customary for a king to be wakened in the morning by a griot singing outside his house.

2064 The white man is Gordon Innes.

CHART I: Sunjata and associates
(as presented by Bamba Suso and Banna Kanute)

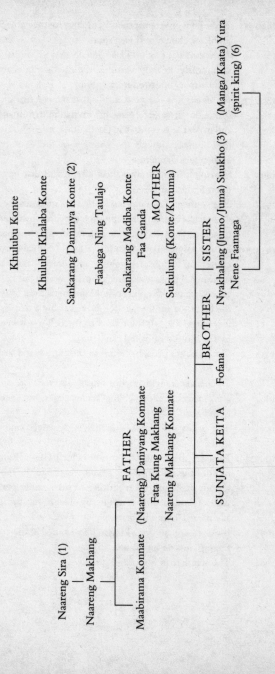

SUNJATA ALSO KNOWN AS:

(Naarena/Naareng/Makhara) Makhang Konnate (4)

Sukulung Jata, Sukulung Yammaru (5)

Sunjate Konnate, Makhang Sunjata

Haimaru and Yammaru

RIVALS/ALLIES

Tamaga Jonding Keya, ancestor of the Darbos

Faring ('powerful') Burema Tunkara, also known as Mansa (king) Farang Tunkara – king of Neema

ALLIES

Military commanders: Kuran Karang Kama Fofana, Tira Makhang, Suru Bande Makhang Kamara

Faa Koli Dumbuya, Sumanguru's nephew, who defects to Sunjata's side

GRIOT

Bala Faasigi/Faaseega Kuyate

OTHER

Sorakhata Bunjafar (emissary)

FOOTNOTES

(1) Naarena, a village south west of Sibi

(2) the Kontes are originally from the Sankarang region, therefore Sankarang is often used as a part of their name

(3) Suukho = female version of 'Keita'

(4) also used for Sunjata's father in Banna Kanute's version

(5) also used for Sunjata's mother in Banna Kanute's version

(6) married to Nene Faamaga in Banna Kanute's version

CHART 2: Sumanguru and associates
(as presented by Bamba Suso and Banna Kanute)

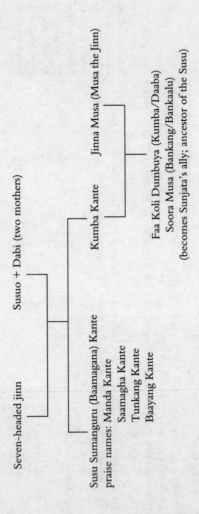

Susuo + Dabi (two mothers)

Seven-headed jinn

Kumba Kante   Jinna Musa (Musa the jinn)

Susu Sumanguru (Baamagana) Kante
praise names: Manda Kante
            Saamagha Kante
            Tunkang Kante
            Baayang Kante

Faa Koli Dumbuya (Kumba/Daaba)
Soora Musa (Bankang/Bankaalu)
(becomes Sunjata's ally; ancestor of the Susu)

(Susu – meaning the ethnic group Susu [Sosso], to which Sumanguru belonged)

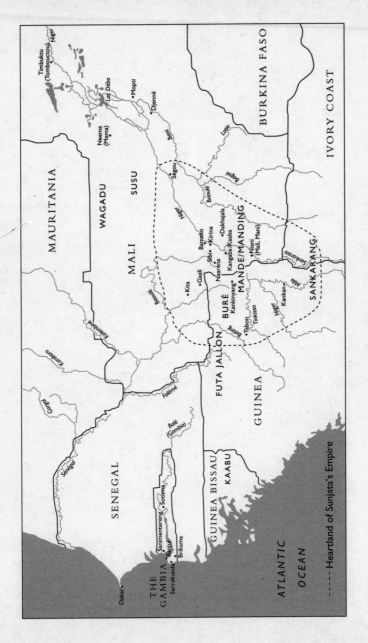

Map: showing places mentioned in the text

PENGUIN CLASSICS

www.penguinclassics.com

- *Details about every Penguin Classic*

- *Advanced information about forthcoming titles*

- *Hundreds of author biographies*

- *FREE resources including critical essays on the books and their historical background, reader's and teacher's guides.*

- *Links to other web resources for the Classics*

- *Discussion area*

- *Online review copy ordering for academics*

- *Competitions with prizes, and challenging Classics trivia quizzes*

READ MORE IN PENGUIN

In every corner of the world, on every subject under the sun, Penguin represents quality and variety – the very best in publishing today.

For complete information about books available from Penguin – including Puffins, Penguin Classics and Arkana – and how to order them, write to us at the appropriate address below. Please note that for copyright reasons the selection of books varies from country to country.

In the United Kingdom: Please write to *Dept. EP, Penguin Books Ltd, Bath Road, Harmondsworth, West Drayton, Middlesex UB7 ODA*

In the United States: Please write to *Consumer Sales, Penguin Putnam Inc., P.O. Box 12289 Dept. B, Newark, New Jersey 07101-5289.* VISA and MasterCard holders call 1-800-788-6262 to order Penguin titles

In Canada: Please write to *Penguin Books Canada Ltd, 10 Alcorn Avenue, Suite 300, Toronto, Ontario M4V 3B2*

In Australia: Please write to *Penguin Books Australia Ltd, P.O. Box 257, Ringwood, Victoria 3134*

In New Zealand: Please write to *Penguin Books (NZ) Ltd, Private Bag 102902, North Shore Mail Centre, Auckland 10*

In India: Please write to *Penguin Books India Pvt Ltd, 11 Community Centre, Panchsheel Park, New Delhi 110017*

In the Netherlands: Please write to *Penguin Books Netherlands bv, Postbus 3507, NL-1001 AH Amsterdam*

In Germany: Please write to *Penguin Books Deutschland GmbH, Metzlerstrasse 26, 60594 Frankfurt am Main*

In Spain: Please write to *Penguin Books S. A., Bravo Murillo 19, 1° B, 28015 Madrid*

In Italy: Please write to *Penguin Italia s.r.l., Via Benedetto Croce 2, 20094 Corsico, Milano*

In France: Please write to *Penguin France, Le Carré Wilson, 62 rue Benjamin Baillaud, 31500 Toulouse*

In Japan: Please write to *Penguin Books Japan Ltd, Kaneko Building, 2-3-25 Koraku, Bunkyo-Ku, Tokyo 112*

In South Africa: Please write to *Penguin Books South Africa (Pty) Ltd, Private Bag X14, Parkview, 2122 Johannesburg*

READ MORE IN PENGUIN

A CHOICE OF CLASSICS

Basho	**The Narrow Road to the Deep North**
	On Love and Barley
Cao Xueqin	**The Story of the Stone** also known as **The Dream of The Red Chamber** (in five volumes)
Confucius	**The Analects**
Khayyam	**The Ruba'iyat of Omar Khayyam**
Lao Tzu	**Tao Te Ching**
Li Po/Tu Fu	**Poems**
Shikibu Murasaki	**The Tale of Genji**
Sarma	**The Pancatantra**
Sei Shonagon	**The Pillow Book of Sei Shonagon**
Somadeva	**Tales from the Kathasaritsagara**
Wu Ch'Eng-En	**Monkey**

ANTHOLOGIES AND ANONYMOUS WORKS

The Bhagavad Gita
Buddhist Scriptures
Chinese Love Poetry
The Dhammapada
Hindu Myths
Japanese No Dramas
The Koran
The Laws of Manu
Poems from the Sanskrit
Poems of the Late T'Ang
The Rig Veda
Speaking of Siva
Tales from the Thousand and One Nights
The Upanishads